REVOLUTIONARY
and
NAPOLEONIC WARS

HISTORY OF WARFARE

Donald Sommerville

RSVP

RAINTREE
STECK-VAUGHN
PUBLISHERS
A Steck-Vaughn Company

Steck-Vaughn Company

First published 1999 by Raintree Steck-Vaughn Publishers,
an imprint of Steck-Vaughn Company.
Copyright © 1999 Brown Partworks Limited.

Library of Congress Cataloging-in-Publication Data

Sommerville, Donald
    Revolutionary and Napoleonic Wars.
       p.   cm. — (History of warfare)
    Includes bibliographical references and index.
    Summary: Examines the wars fought from the latter 1700s through the mid-1800s, describing changes in the make-up of the armies, fighting tactics, and weaponry used.
    ISBN 0-8172-5446-3
    1. Revolutionaries — Juvenile literature.   2. Military history, Modern — 18th century — Juvenile literature.   3. Military history, Modern — 19th century — Juvenile literature.   4. Napoleonic Wars, 1800–1815 — Juvenile literature.   [1. Military history, Modern — 18th century.   2. Military history, Modern — 19th century.]   I. Title.   II. Series: History of warfare (Austin, Tex.)
D288.W467   1999
904'.7 — dc21

                                              98-6669
                                            CIP
                                            AC

Printed and bound in the United States
1 2 3 4 5 6 7 8 9 0 IP 03 02 01 00 99 98

Brown Partworks Limited
Managing Editor: Ian Westwell
Senior Designer: Paul Griffin
Picture Researcher: Wendy Verren
Editorial Assistant: Antony Shaw
Cartographers: William le Bihan, John See
Index: Pat Coward

Raintree Steck-Vaughn
Publishing Director: Walter Kossmann
Project Manager: Joyce Spicer
Editor: Shirley Shalit

Front cover: George Washington at the Battle of Monmouth in 1778 (main picture) and the abdication of Emperor Napoleon, 1814 (inset).
Page 1: The U.S. bombardment of Veracruz, Mexico, 1847.

Consultant
Dr. Niall Barr, Senior Lecturer,
Royal Military Academy Sandhurst,
Camberley, Surrey, England

CONTENTS

INTRODUCTION

This volume looks at the history of warfare from the last decades of the 18th century to the middle of the 19th century. Warfare during this period saw only a few technical advances. The smoothbore flintlock musket was still the standard infantry arm, although the rifled musket with its longer range and greater accuracy was becoming increasingly important.

Cannon were more mobile than ever before, but their range and accuracy were little improved. Cavalry was used for two main purposes. First, heavy cavalry, partly armored men on large horses, delivered battlefield charges. Second, light cavalrymen, mounted on smaller horses armed with short muskets (carbines), were used to harass the enemy and for scouting.

On land Napoleon Bonaparte dominated the conduct of warfare. His greatest ability was his strategic vision. His chief aim was always to use rapid movement to bring his enemy to battle on unequal terms. Napoleon often faced numerically superior foes and always attempted to destroy them one by one before they could unite against him.

Speed of movement was absolutely essential to his plans. Typically, Napoleon would use speed and deception to march around behind an enemy army, thereby cutting its lines of communication and leaving it at a distinct disadvantage.

Perhaps the greatest change of the era was in the structure of the armies. These changes did not begin with Napoleon, but he established a system that remains to the present. The usual infantry division, about 10,000 men divided between a number of brigades (usually three), was developed by the French in the mid-18th century.

In the 1790s the French modified their divisions to include not just infantry but cavalry and artillery as well. These divisions had all the weapons and troop types to fight independently. Napoleon combined divisions, usually three or four, to form corps of around 30,000 men. These were, in effect, small armies.

On campaign these corps moved independently but could be brought together rapidly if necessary. Few of Napoleon's many opponents could match his speed of maneuver and the rapid gathering of his separate corps. One of Napoleon's favorite war strategies was to concentrate his corps between two enemy armies and then move rapidly against one before it could link up with the other. Although his foes had more troops, Napoleon would often have greater numbers on the battlefield.

Armies in the age of Napoleon were becoming increasingly bigger. Farms were able to supply large armies with food, and manufacturers could provide the weapons and clothing they needed.

The impact of this "industrialization" of warfare was matched, particularly in France and the United States, by a widespread popular belief that wars were worth fighting. People, who in the past saw war as being of little value to anyone but their rulers, increasingly fought for ideals, particularly liberty and democracy.

4

THE AMERICAN REVOLUTION

The American Revolution confirmed that a new nation would be formed from the 13 British colonies along the eastern seaboard of the North American continent. The principal cause of the revolution was summed up in the slogan "no taxation without representation." The British government claimed to be able to pass laws and impose taxes on the American colonies, even though the Americans did not have any representatives serving in the British Parliament. This lack of democracy would lead to war in 1775.

The British people had a large national debt and the taxes they paid at home were high. They knew that these taxes were in place largely because of the expense of wars to protect the colonies and the costs of defending them. The British thought that it was about time the prosperous colonies were made to pay their share through taxes. Unfortunately for the British they chose to set about this in a way that led to resentment and then war.

The Intolerable Acts

At the end of 1773 a group of Bostonians staged a protest against the tea tax, tipping the tea cargoes of three ships into the city's harbor. This "Boston Tea Party" was copied in other American ports and provoked the British government into retaliating. Harsh new laws, known in America as the Intolerable Acts, were passed in London. A force of some 3,000 British troops was sent

British troops and colonial minutemen (militia) exchange musket fire at Lexington on April 19, 1775. This incident, which left eight colonists dead and a further ten wounded, marked the beginning of the American Revolution.

to Boston to help enforce them. The laws were mainly meant to apply to Massachusetts, the most rebellious colony. However, all the American colonies joined in protesting against them in a Continental Congress (revolutionary government) that met for the first time in Philadelphia in September 1774.

The opening shots

The spark that set off the fighting followed in April 1775. British troops from Boston tried to seize supplies from the colonial militia a few miles inland at Lexington and Concord. Local militiamen, known as minutemen because they were supposed to be ready for action at a minute's notice, fought back and the British had to retreat to Boston. No one really knows who fired the first shot on Lexington Common, but when the day's fighting was over the British had suffered 273 casualties, including 73 dead. The minutemen, fighting from cover, suffered a total of 93 men killed, wounded, and missing.

The people and government of Massachusetts were outraged. The Massachusetts militia besieged the British army in Boston. Militiamen from other New England colonies soon joined in. In June the Continental Congress appointed a Virginia militia officer, George Washington, to take command.

Despite the enthusiasm with which some Americans took up their cause, it was hard to judge which side was better placed to win the war. Many Americans wanted to remain loyal to Britain. About 500,000 Americans, one in five of the white population, were Loyalists, or Tories as they were also known, and others quietly favored the British side. About 20,000 Americans eventually fought in Loyalist units and others joined the British forces.

The rival forces

Britain had other advantages, too. The British army was relatively small, but it was well trained by the standards of the time. It was supported by the world's largest navy and the money generated by the large British economy and an overseas empire.

However, the America colonies were some 3,000 miles (4,800 km) from Britain and this distance was the colonists' greatest advantage. The colonial armies often had problems keeping their soldiers serving for more than a few months before they returned home, but even when they did they could usually be replaced by other local recruits. Over 200,000 men eventually fought at one time or another on the American side.

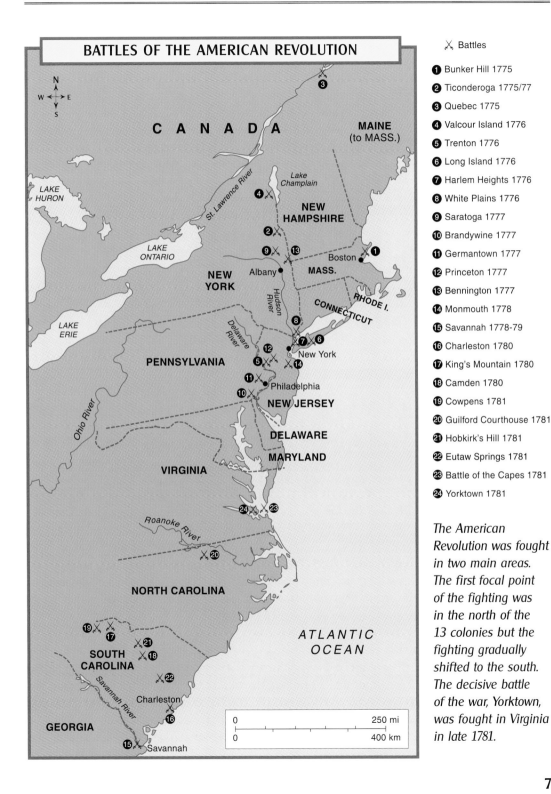

BATTLES OF THE AMERICAN REVOLUTION

✗ Battles

1. Bunker Hill 1775
2. Ticonderoga 1775/77
3. Quebec 1775
4. Valcour Island 1776
5. Trenton 1776
6. Long Island 1776
7. Harlem Heights 1776
8. White Plains 1776
9. Saratoga 1777
10. Brandywine 1777
11. Germantown 1777
12. Princeton 1777
13. Bennington 1777
14. Monmouth 1778
15. Savannah 1778-79
16. Charleston 1780
17. King's Mountain 1780
18. Camden 1780
19. Cowpens 1781
20. Guilford Courthouse 1781
21. Hobkirk's Hill 1781
22. Eutaw Springs 1781
23. Battle of the Capes 1781
24. Yorktown 1781

The American Revolution was fought in two main areas. The first focal point of the fighting was in the north of the 13 colonies but the fighting gradually shifted to the south. The decisive battle of the war, Yorktown, was fought in Virginia in late 1781.

THE HUNTING RIFLE

The standard military firearm in all countries throughout the 18th century was the smoothbore musket. However, a small number of troops using a different type of weapon, the rifle, played an important part among the American forces.

Rifles were more accurate than muskets because of grooves cut into the inside of the barrel. These imparted spin to the musket ball, giving it greater accuracy.

With a musket even an expert was unlikely to hit a single enemy at more than about 100 yards (91 m). Riflemen could pick off enemy officers or sentries at 200 yards (183 m) or more. Hunting rifles enabled American forces to inflict often heavy long-range casualties on the British.

American soldiers armed with hunting rifles practice their marksmanship.

The whole British army in 1776 was less than 100,000 strong, although it was expanded later. Replacements for any British soldier killed, wounded, or captured in America had to come a very long way. This helped make the British generals cautious and careful. The British also had to bring nearly all their supplies an equally long distance. If they tried to get what they needed in America by living off the land, they risked undermining the support of the pro-British Loyalists.

About one-sixth of the colonial population was made up of slaves and at times the British tried to expand their forces by offering freedom to slaves who would fight on their side. Again the British had to be careful since Loyalists were concentrated in the southern colonies and might switch to the American side rather than lose their slaves. Some freed slaves also fought on the American side, but most white Americans on either side did not want slaves to be armed or freed.

Distance from British bases was not necessarily a deciding factor since Britain had fought and won distant colonial wars on many occasions in the past. However, on those occasions the enemy usually presented a clear target for attack, perhaps a capital city or a group of major fortresses. America had no vital strategic center to attack in this way.

Britain fights alone

In previous wars Britain could usually count on help from various European allies. This time Britain had to fight other European countries who had supported or been backed by Britain during many earlier 18th century conflicts. This lack of allies meant that Britain had to defend itself in Europe and in its other colonies.

Possessions in India and the Caribbean were far more valuable to the British than the American colonies. The British were ready to put more resources into defending these than in fighting in America. After France allied with the Americans in 1778, Britain's main concern was not the fight against the American colonists as much as it was the war against France.

British leaders proved to be poor at developing plans and coordinating their scattered forces to overcome these disadvantages. America's leaders made better use of their resources. George Washington developed into an exceptional and inspiring military leader and many of his junior commanders became tough and resourceful fighters.

Most Americans were accustomed to using guns for hunting and so had what was effectively sufficient military skill and fieldcraft to be able to join in an attack on a British outpost or supply column. Fighting in a formal battle was a different matter. But with good leadership and training, supplied in part by several foreign experts, the techniques needed for a formal battle could be learned.

The opening battles

On June 17, 1775, two days after Washington's appointment to command the army at Boston and before he had arrived to take up his post, the British mounted an attack against their besiegers around Boston. American troops had begun to dig in on hills overlooking

British troops storm the American defenses during the Battle of Bunker Hill, June 17, 1775. The British infantry forced the American militia to retreat after some hard fighting but suffered nearly 50 percent casualties.

WASHINGTON AND THE CONTINENTAL ARMY

George Washington began his military career with the Virginia militia during the French and Indian Wars between 1754 and 1763. In June 1775 Congress appointed him to lead the first national American army, the Continental Army.

Washington commanded the army throughout the war. His greatest achievements were as an organizer of colonial forces and as the inspirational figurehead of revolution. He turned the army into a well-organized force, despite difficulties with supplies, recruitment, and political squabbles between the colonies.

Washington's battle generalship was not always so successful. His forces were defeated on Long Island in 1776 because he positioned them badly, for example. But his skills as a general did improve with experience. Later in the war he did better at coordinating the various French and American armies that won the decisive victory at Yorktown in 1781.

In 1789 Washington was elected as first president of the newly constituted United States and served until 1797. He worked hard to give the presidency a clear role in the new nation.

Boston from across the Charles River to the north. The British decided to drive them away. The battle that followed is usually called the Battle of Bunker Hill, even though the main fighting took place on the slopes of nearby Breed's Hill.

The British advanced on the American defenses. Two attacks were thrown back with severe casualties. A third British advance did make the Americans retreat, but the British were exhausted. The British lost more than 1,000 men killed or wounded out of a force of 2,500. American casualties were about 400.

The main result of the battle was that the largest British force in America remained besieged in Boston for the rest of the year, while most of New England came under the control of the Americans. The British even had to evacuate Boston in March 1776. They never returned.

American forces attacked north from New York and Maine into British Canada late in 1775. However, by early 1776 the invasion was defeated. The British tried to attack from Canada but advanced slowly. In October the British won the Battle of Valcour Island on Lake Champlain but could go no farther.

The main British forces in America were more successful in 1776. These were now under the command of two brothers, General Sir William Howe and Admiral Lord Richard Howe.

Their orders were to take New York. The British began landing a force of some 32,000 men on Staten Island in July. These included 9,000 German Hessian mercenaries fighting for the British.

Washington was based on Manhattan Island but also deployed troops on Long Island. General Howe attacked and defeated Washington's men in the Battle of Long Island on August 27. Washington then had to evacuate New York after defeats at Harlem Heights (September 16) and White Plains (October 28). He and the army fell back to Pennsylvania. Congress had issued the Declaration of Independence on July 4, 1776, but with these British victories it seemed America's revolution was in trouble.

Morale-raising victory

Washington struck back with a surprise crossing of the Delaware River and a successful attack on part of the British force at Trenton, New Jersey, on December 26. This gave his army new confidence to fight on. Washington was not yet ready to fight the main British force, however. By clever maneuvering he avoided being pinned down by Howe throughout the spring and early summer of 1777.

The British government had grander plans for the rest of the year. Lord George Germain, the British colonial secretary based in London, was in charge of British operations. He devised a

Washington leads his army across the Delaware River from New Jersey to Pennsylvania on December 11, 1776. He recrossed the river 14 days later. This move, carried out in the depths of winter, surprised the British and enabled Washington to win a morale-raising victory at Trenton.

strategy for General John Burgoyne to attack south from Canada toward Albany, New York, while Howe moved part of his army north from New York to link up with Burgoyne. This move would divide the American colonies in two.

Major British defeats

The idea looked good on paper in London but for it to succeed it needed the British commanders to work together properly. Howe and Burgoyne did not coordinate their plans and Germain did not give them clear orders to stay in touch. Burgoyne was left to stumble to defeat at Saratoga in the fall of 1777.

Instead of helping Burgoyne, Howe had moved his army south from New York by sea to Chesapeake Bay to strike at Philadelphia. General Washington and his men tried to defend

THE SARATOGA CAMPAIGN

The Saratoga campaign of 1777 was the first clear and substantial American victory of the war. It persuaded France to ally with the Americans and made it certain that the war would be a prolonged struggle that Britain could easily lose.

General John Burgoyne moved his British army south from Canada and captured Fort Ticonderoga in July, aiming to link up with British forces in New York. He pushed on farther the next month. In August he learned that General William Howe would not be moving up from New York to support him, but Burgoyne decided not to turn back.

In September Burgoyne and his men crossed the Hudson River and attacked the main American forces near Saratoga. There were two phases in this engagement, the Battle of Freeman's Farm on September 19 and the Battle of Bemis Heights on October 7. Both of these British attacks on the American lines were beaten back with heavy casualties. The British were now outnumbered, and on October 17 Burgoyne and his 6,000 troops surrendered to the American commander, General Horatio Gates.

American forces attack a fort held by Hessian (German) troops during the Battle of Saratoga. The officer falling wounded from his horse is General Benedict Arnold.

JOHN PAUL JONES

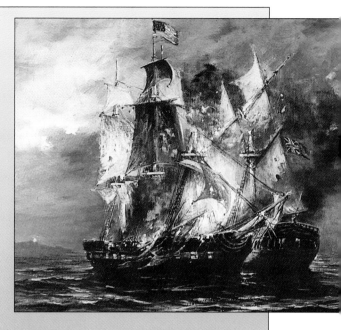

John Paul Jones was the most famous early leader of what is now the U. S. Navy. He was born in Scotland as John Paul but changed his name after being involved in a killing in Tobago in the West Indies in 1773. Jones moved to America and then became an officer in the Continental Navy soon after it was established in 1775.

In 1777 Jones was appointed captain of the *Ranger* and set off for European waters. He carried out raids on the British coast during 1778 and captured the British warship *Drake* after a tough fight.

In 1779 Jones switched to a converted trading vessel called the *Bonhomme Richard.* His most famous exploit came in the Battle of Flamborough Head off the northeast coast of England on September 23, 1779. A three-hour point-blank struggle ended with the British ship *Serapis* surrendering to Jones. The *Bonhomme Richard* was so badly damaged that it sank two days later.

Subsequently Jones returned to America but the war ended before he was given another ship. In later life he served for a time in the Russian navy. He died in France but is now buried at the U.S. Naval Academy at Annapolis, Maryland.

The Bonhomme Richard *(left) in flames and sinking during John Paul Jones's epic three-hour battle with the* Serapis *in September 1779.*

Philadelphia but were defeated in the Battle of the Brandywine on September 11, 1777. Howe captured Philadelphia on September 26. Philadelphia had been the American capital up to this point, but if Howe hoped that capturing it would discourage the rebels, he was disappointed. On October 4 Washington attacked the British in the Battle of Germantown.

Soon after this both armies decided to move into winter quarters to conserve their strength for the next year. Washington's force was at a particularly low ebb. His men were almost starving and many had no shoes or any warm clothing. Over 2,000 American troops died from the harsh conditions that winter. Even so a turning point had been reached. A German adviser,

Baron Friedrich von Steuben, arrived in the Continental Army camp at Valley Forge, Pennsylvania, and his training helped a great deal, turning the army into a fully-trained force.

America's European allies

Even more important, when news reached Europe of the victory at Saratoga and of Washington's continued resistance, France began discussions for an alliance with American representatives. The alliance was agreed on in February 1778 and war between Britain and France followed in June.

A year later, in June 1779, Spain declared war on Britain and at the end of 1780 Britain and the Netherlands also went to war. The British navy would no longer have a free hand in transporting troops and supplies along the American eastern seaboard. It would have to counter the threats from the Dutch and Spanish. The overstretched British navy and army would have less chance to take the initiative in the American colonies.

The French alliance did not have an impact immediately. France, like Britain, had other interests. In 1778, for example, a French fleet helped an American expedition attack Newport, Rhode Island, but did not stay long before sailing away to fight the British over the sugar-producing islands in the Caribbean.

From 1778 through 1782 the British and French each made various attacks on enemy-held islands. Dominica, St. Lucia, and Grenada were among those that changed hands at various times. There were several naval battles with indecisive results until the British finally won the Battle of the Saintes, fought off the island of Dominica in the Caribbean in April 1782.

Even if the French did not make much direct contribution in America at first, their alliance immediately produced a change in British plans. General Henry Clinton took over as the British commander-in-chief and was ordered to pull out of Philadelphia and move his main force to New York.

The war in the south

The Battle of Monmouth in New Jersey on June 28 was the one major battle in 1778. Neither side won a clear victory. Casualties were about even but for the first time the American forces proved able to meet the British regulars on level terms in an open battle.

After the Battle of Monmouth, Clinton's forces continued on their way to New York, followed by Washington's men. The British held New York for the remainder of the war but they did

not make any important land attacks from their base there. From this point on the British abandoned their attempts to bring the middle colonies and New England back under their control. They pinned their hopes on making gains in the south.

The British began their southern campaign in Georgia. Some of Clinton's men attacked and captured Savannah at the end of December 1778. Other British forces moved up from Florida to join the fighting. By the summer of 1779 American troops in Georgia had been reinforced and were joined by a French army and naval fleet. Together these besieged the British in Savannah. Through September and October the town held out. Eventually the French and Americans gave up the siege. The French ships were forced to sail away because of worries about them being damaged by winter storms.

More British successes followed in 1780. They captured Charleston, South Carolina, after a siege that lasted from February to May and won an important battle at Camden in August. But the British, now commanded by General Charles

British and American forces clash during the Battle of Camden, South Carolina, August 16, 1780. The battle was a disaster for the Americans. They lost 900 men killed out of an army of 3,000. Among the casualties was Baron de Kalb, seen here lying mortally wounded on the ground (center). De Kalb was a French volunteer fighting with the Americans.

The Battle of King's Mountain, in South Carolina, October 7, 1780, was unique in the American Revolution. All of the troops involved were American. The battle ended when the pro-British Loyalists were routed with heavy casualties by the colonial militia.

Cornwallis, discovered that winning major battles was not the whole story. Any detachments from their main army were liable to be caught and heavily defeated. A force of Tory Loyalists was wiped out in this way at King's Mountain in October 1780 and a division of the main British army badly beaten at Cowpens in northern South Carolina on January 17, 1781.

The final battle

The new American commander in the south, General Nathanael Greene, fought a drawn battle with Cornwallis at Guilford Courthouse, North Carolina, in March 1781. This battle was enough to persuade Cornwallis that he had to give up his efforts to hold Georgia and the Carolinas. Cornwallis marched north into Virginia. By August 1781 he had established a base at Yorktown. It was soon besieged.

The crushing French and American victory at Yorktown in October decided the outcome of the war in America. The British still held New York but they had clearly no chance of regaining control of any other part of their former colonies. A new British government came to power in March 1782 and asked for peace. The Treaty of Paris was agreed on in November 1782 and finally signed on November 30, 1783. The United States was recognized as an independent nation.

Counting the cost

The American Revolution was the longest war in American history until the Vietnam War. It was also very costly in human lives. About 26,000 American soldiers died, roughly one percent of the population. In common with every war before the 20th century many—about 18,000—of the deaths were from disease, hunger, cold, and other non-battle causes.

The casualties and their grieving families were not the only sufferers, however. Besides the inevitable destruction of homes and property, about 100,000 pro-British Loyalist refugees left the former colonies during the war itself or shortly afterward to begin new lives in Canada or elsewhere. The new United States had had a harsh and difficult birth.

THE BATTLE OF YORKTOWN

When General Cornwallis established a British base at Yorktown, Virginia, in the summer of 1781 both sides recognized it was a crucial stage of the war. With his French allies General Washington decided to attack Yorktown. Washington led most of his army overland toward Chesapeake Bay. At the end of August he was reinforced by 3,000 more French troops and a fleet from the Caribbean.

The British had about 8,000 men to defend the town; Washington now had 9,500 Americans and 7,800 French. The British navy tried to help but returned to its base at New York after being badly damaged by a French fleet at the Battle of the Virginia Capes in early September.

There could now be only one result. Washington's men brought their guns into range of the town at the end of September and began to pound the British defenses. On October 19 Cornwallis surrendered what remained of the garrison.

The American victory at Yorktown confirmed that Britain had lost the struggle to retain control of its distant American colonies. Yorktown was the decisive battle of the war.

The Yorktown campaign demonstrated that the American army had come a long way since it was created on July 3, 1775. The victory at Yorktown was due in large part to the army's professionalism and battlefield experience.

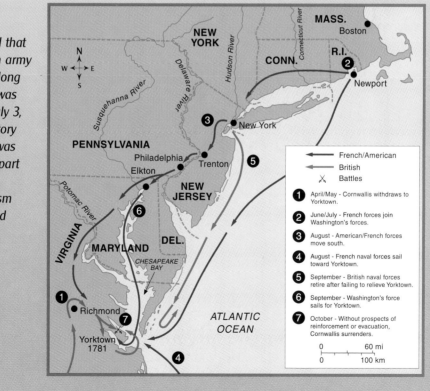

French/American
British
Battles

1 April/May - Cornwallis withdraws to Yorktown.
2 June/July - French forces join Washington's forces.
3 August - American/French forces move south.
4 August - French naval forces sail toward Yorktown.
5 September - British naval forces retire after failing to relieve Yorktown.
6 September - Washington's force sails for Yorktown.
7 October - Without prospects of reinforcement or evacuation, Cornwallis surrenders.

0 60 mi
0 100 km

FRANCE'S REVOLUTIONARY WARS

By the 1780s France was still the most powerful country in Europe but the harsh government of King Louis XVI was unpopular. In 1789 the French Revolution began and a new National Assembly took control of the country from the king and his government. The National Assembly published the Declaration of the Rights of Man, stating that all men were equal and that the authority of government could only come from the people as a whole, not from kings or other traditional leaders in the nobility or the Church.

The French army, made up of poorly trained conscripts, defeats a Prussian force at Valmy on September 30, 1792. Heavy French cannon fire forced the Prussians to retreat.

These ideas were truly revolutionary because they threatened to change the whole organization of government and society not only within France but in other countries in Europe as well. Governments elsewhere found these political ideas a threat to their power and tried to prevent such views from spreading to their countries. The French revolutionaries, on the other hand, were scared that foreign rulers wanted to restore the old style of undemocratic rule in France. This led to tension and in April 1792 the French declared war on Austria and Prussia.

REVOLUTIONARY WARFARE

Before the French Revolution armies in Europe and in ex-European colonies, like the United States, had usually been made up of long-serving professional soldiers. In times of emergency they were occasionally backed up by local militias. These temporary troops usually had little military training and tended to be rather second-rate soldiers.

The French Revolution brought about a radical change to this pattern. After the revolution countries increasingly tried to give military training to all their young men in times of peace and mobilize as many of them as possible in times of war.

In the early stages of the French Revolution many of the French soldiers were enthusiastic volunteers. Although many were not professional soldiers, they were determined to fight against the trained soldiers of other European countries to preserve their new freedom.

France's first national army was raised under a law of 1793, which summed up this new trend toward all-out war: "Young men shall fight; married men shall make weapons and transport supplies; women will make tents and clothes and will serve in the hospitals; children will convert old linen into bandages; old men will have themselves carried into the public squares to make speeches to inspire the soldiers, to preach hatred against kings, and proclaim the unity of the republic."

Now the other European countries were afraid of France's military aggression and soon came to worry about France's growing power to dominate Europe. However, it was not until 1793 that several were prepared to unite against France. As the opening stages of the war confirmed, none of them was strong enough militarily to defeat France alone.

Little real fighting

When war began in 1792, it seemed as if France would quickly be beaten. The army of the revolutionary government was disorganized and its soldiers badly trained. Prussian troops captured towns and fortresses in northeast France. But the Prussians moved very slowly, giving the French time to put together an

LAZARE NICOLAS CARNOT

Lazare Carnot was an engineer officer in the French army before the revolution. He was elected to the revolutionary parliaments in 1791 and 1792 and voted for the execution of King Louis. Later, in 1793, he joined the Committee of Public Safety and set about turning France's new national army into an effective fighting force. He became known as the "organizer of victory" because of the successful methods he devised.

Carnot remained in the various French governments until 1797 and was made minister of war by Napoleon Bonaparte to help support the military campaigns of 1800–01.

After Napoleon made himself emperor in 1804, Carnot retired to write books on the science of fortification. He became minister of the interior during the final Napoleonic campaign in 1815 and then went into exile after Napoleon's defeat at Waterloo.

army to oppose them. The two armies met at Valmy, France, on September 20, 1792. There was little real fighting during the battle but enough to persuade the Prussians to retreat. A few weeks later the French won a second battle, this time against the Austrians at Jemappes (now in Belgium). Together these two battles gave France a breathing space.

Two days after the Battle of Valmy the revolutionaries declared France a republic. King Louis XVI was executed in January 1793 as the most ruthless of France's new leaders took control of the revolution. This horrified many other European countries. Britain, Spain, and Holland joined Austria and Prussia in an anti-French alliance known as the First Coalition.

Mass conscription

The allies of the First Coalition gained the upper hand in the fighting in the first half of 1793. France's government, the Committee of Public Safety, responded with two sets of measures. It declared the *levée en masse* (mass conscription). Under this order every adult Frenchman was liable to military service. To make sure that this was obeyed, the committee introduced laws that made it virtually impossible for Frenchmen to escape being called up into the army.

Many in the new mass armies were enthusiastic about fighting for France, believing they were part of a new, democratic country. They believed they were fighting for a worthwhile cause. The soldiers quickly became veterans. Because they gave up old-fashioned ideas about rigid battlefield drill, they learned to outmaneuver and outfight their enemies who stuck to the old methods.

In the new French army anyone could become an officer or a general, not just the lords and nobility as in the past. Many of the new officers proved themselves daring and courageous in battle and quickly rose to the top ranks where they showed vigorous and dynamic leadership. In Paris, because of his great military knowledge, Lazare Nicolas Carnot created a framework of military organization and discipline to complete the process that made the French army the most effective in the world.

All this began to pay off in late 1793. The French defeated attempts to invade northern and eastern France. More French victories followed in 1794. In the first months of 1795 they over-ran Holland. That was enough for Prussia, Holland, Spain, and some German countries. They made peace with France, leaving Britain and Austria to fight on.

Napoleon's first action

A new government, known as the Directory, took over in France in mid-1795 and successfully put down an uprising in Paris later in the year. During this revolt the government forces were led by a young artillery officer called Napoleon Bonaparte. Bonaparte had already distinguished himself by using shore-based artillery to beat off an Anglo-Spanish fleet supporting the royalist-held

Bonaparte (at right with telescope) oversees the defeat of the Anglo-Spanish fleet in the harbor of Toulon in 1793.

THE BATTLE OF RIVOLI

In the second half of 1796 and at the start of 1797 the fighting in Italy was centered around the Austrian-held town of Mantua. The French were besieging the town and the Austrians sent armies to defeat the siege and beat the French.

In January 1797 Bonaparte was taken by surprise when the Austrians attacked. His units were too far apart and were only just able to link up at Rivoli, northeast of Mantua, in time. Even so the Austrians still outnumbered the French by 28,000 to 15,000 at the start of the battle on January 14, though some 5,000 more French reinforcements arrived during the day.

The Austrians wasted their advantage by splitting their attack into six columns. They never made their superior numbers count because they could not all be coordinated to attack at the same time in the difficult hill terrain. The French smashed two of the six attacks on the first day and held the others off.

Napoleon was so confident of victory that he left taking part of his army to attack another Austrian force, and leaving his subordinate, General Barthélemy Joubert, to complete the victory on the 15th. Joubert captured 11,000 prisoners; Bonaparte won another battle on the 16th and Mantua surrendered on February 2.

Bonaparte (mounted on the white horse) receives news that his French forces have smashed the Austrians at Rivoli.

port of Toulon, which was besieged by revolutionary forces from August to September 1793. Fighting continued in both Germany and northern Italy. In early 1796 Bonaparte got his reward from the French government—he was appointed to command the French army in Italy.

Bonaparte had joined the French army before the revolution and was promoted when he showed his abilities in the fighting in 1793 and 1794. Before he was given his new command in 1796, Napoleon was one of many rising stars. Within months, however, he became a national hero.

Austria's best general, Archduke Charles, won several battles against French forces in Germany throughout 1796 but any importance these might have had was more than counterbalanced by Bonaparte's astonishing successes in Italy. The soldiers of the French army in Italy were hungry and dressed in little more than rags. Somehow Bonaparte inspired them to carry out a rapid and devastating series of attacks.

The enemy forces were made up of Austrians and the army of the Kingdom of Sardinia, which included the part of northern Italy known as Piedmont. Bonaparte maneuvered between the two armies and then used his full strength to beat them one at a time. He then repeated the strategy to defeat other Austrian armies. Bonaparte's victories in 1796 included Montenotte (April 12), Lodi (May 10), Castiglione (August 5), Bassano (September 8), and Arcola (November 15–17).

Bonaparte's Egyptian campaign

By January 1797 an Austrian force was besieged in the town of Mantua. The Austrians sent a relief army but it was defeated at Rivoli, northeast of Mantua, on the 14th. By March the French were advancing across the Alps. Austria agreed to make peace.

France wanted to invade Britain but British naval supremacy made this impossible. Instead Bonaparte led a French expedition to invade Egypt, hoping to carve out an empire for France and threaten Britain's most valuable colonies in India. The French landed in Egypt in July 1798. They easily defeated the inefficient Egyptian armies but they were soon cut off by the British fleet.

The campaigns fought by Bonaparte in northern Italy from March 1796 to late 1797 were astounding. He outfought and outmaneuvered larger enemy armies, winning many battles. His victories made sure that revolutionary France was safe from invasion from the southeast.

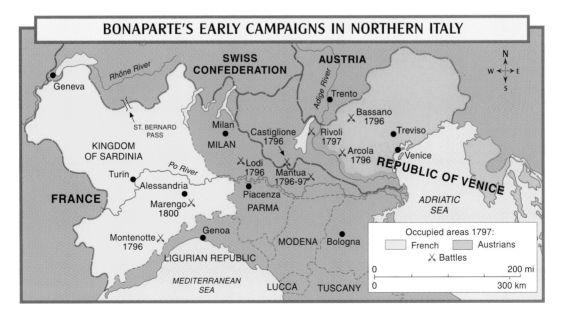

BONAPARTE'S EARLY CAMPAIGNS IN NORTHERN ITALY

The Battle of Marengo on June 14, 1800, began badly for Bonaparte. Here, he is trying to rally his retreating troops, who have been pushed back by superior Austrian forces. Bonaparte was successful and went on to win the battle.

Bonaparte escaped back to France in a small, fast warship in October 1798, leaving his army behind. The survivors, some 26,000 troops under General Jacques de Menou, eventually surrendered to the British in 1801.

While Bonaparte was away in Egypt, France's enemies created a new alliance. Russia, Britain, and Austria were the main partners in this Second Coalition. The alliance members began their attacks early in 1798. Austrian and Russian troops won a series of battles in Italy, reversing the results of the fighting in 1796 and 1797, but the allies were not so successful elsewhere. British troops were withdrawn from Holland, and in Switzerland a French general, André Masséna, defeated the Russians.

Napoleon takes control

As soon as he arrived back in France from Egypt, Bonaparte organized a revolt and had himself appointed head of the French government with the title of First Consul. He took command of the main French army and marched into Italy in May 1800. He led his army over the Alps by the St. Bernard Pass, a route which meant he could attack the Austrians from behind.

The decisive battle was fought at Marengo on June 14. Bonaparte nearly threw away his early advantage by careless maneuvers in the first phase of the battle but French reinforcements arrived just in time. The Austrian army in Italy agreed to an armistice the next day.

While all this was going on, another French general, Jean Victor Moreau, was driving the Austrians back in southern Germany. Moreau smashed an Austrian army at the Battle of Hohenlinden, western Germany, on December 3. Austria was now threatened from the west and south and made peace.

A brief end to hostilities

Britain and France were still at war but could do little to harm each other. Britain could not challenge the French army on land and France could not invade Britain because the British navy was too strong. Faced with a stalemate, the two made peace by signing the Treaty of Amiens in 1802.

Europe was at peace for the first time in ten years. France had been weak in 1792 but was now secure. However, the revolution had counted for little in the end. Bonaparte ruled France like any previous king. He had developed such a liking for power and conquest that it seemed likely that the Treaty of Amiens would be only a temporary truce between Europe's leading powers.

French infantry and cavalry advance against the Austrian lines during the Battle of Hohenlinden on December 3, 1800. The French won due to their speed of maneuver, which allowed them to surround parts of the enemy army.

THE EMPEROR'S FIRST CAMPAIGNS

The Treaty of Amiens in 1802 had given Europe peace for the first time in ten years but it had not solved anything. Old grievances remained. Leaders in all the other major countries distrusted France. All sides dragged their feet when it actually came to carrying out the promises they had made in the treaty. A few months after the treaty Bonaparte was proclaimed Consul for Life and in 1804 had himself crowned as the Emperor Napoleon I of France. He began to plan campaigns against all the other leading European powers.

Napoleon dressed in the costume he wore for his coronation as French emperor on December 2, 1804. The key moment of the ceremony came when Napoleon grabbed the crown from the hands of Pope Pius VII and crowned himself. This action symbolized that he, not the Church or its officials (or the old royal family of France), was the unchallenged head of the French government.

Napoleon concentrated all government authority in France in his own person. He had astonishing stamina and wide interests, which enabled him to complete huge quantities of work. But he also became obsessed with his own glory and destiny. In his increasingly power-mad way he became convinced that what he wanted for himself was automatically the best for France and the rest of Europe.

Napoleon did much to develop life in France, creating a body of law still known as the Napoleonic Code, but he was a soldier at heart. He was careful at first to remain popular at home. Most of France's people were peasant farmers. They were allowed to keep land taken from the aristocracy and the Church during the French Revolution. They would not be so happy later when more and more of their sons were killed in Napoleon's wars, but in 1804 those days were still a little way off.

Napoleon's armies

The French army was an excellent tool for Napoleon's war plans. France's population was as large as Britain's, Prussia's, and Austria's put together, with the military manpower to match. Many of the soldiers were now veteran fighters. They were led by a host of young officers, all made loyal to their emperor by lavish gifts of titles and money. His dashing cavalry commander, Joachim Murat, was even made king of part of Italy in 1808.

Napoleon's wars were hugely expensive. It was part of the secret of his success in his years of triumph that all France's wars were fought on foreign soil. This meant that his armies simply stole their food from the people wherever they happened to be fighting. Napoleon also made defeated governments pay huge sums in "compensation" to France. He used this money to pay his troops and keep the French government wealthy.

The Treaty of Amiens ended in May 1803 and Britain declared war on France. Napoleon devised various impractical plans to invade Britain and assembled a huge army along the

Joachim Murat was one of Napoleon's most important generals. He was renowned for his dashing command of the French cavalry and the extravagance of his clothing.

THE IMPERIAL GUARD

Napoleon's Imperial Guard was the most famous part of his army. It started out as his small personal escort when he was a young general but then mushroomed in size. It included about 12,000 men in 1805 and over 100,000 in 1814. The Guard contained infantry, cavalry, and artillery units.

Guard soldiers were paid much more than troops in ordinary line regiments and they always got the best rations and equipment. It was a great honor to be selected to join the Guard and soldiers had to have had five years' service and to have fought bravely in several battles to be eligible to join.

The Guard usually formed Napoleon's reserve force, ready to win battles by decisive attacks or to block the most dangerous enemy moves. People came to think that the tough veterans of the Guard were invincible, always able to snatch victory from the jaws of defeat. When the Guard's attacks failed at the Battle of Waterloo in 1815, it was a signal to the whole French army that the battle was lost.

French northern coast. These plans were undermined by the British naval triumph at Trafalgar in 1805, but Napoleon had already abandoned them by then.

Britain had no worthwhile allies until 1805, when Austria and Russia joined the Third Coalition. Prussia could not decide what to do and made the mistake of remaining neutral for the moment. Napoleon knew that one Austrian army was in southern Germany. It would take months before their Russian allies could march across Europe to help the Austrians. He attacked while his enemies were divided. At the end of August 1805 Napoleon's Grand Army set off for Germany.

Napoleon's greatest battle

The French outmaneuvered an isolated Austrian army at Ulm in southern Germany and forced it to surrender. Napoleon then urged his men on into Austria. They captured the capital, Vienna, on November 14. Another part of the Austrian army and a larger Russian force under the cautious but shrewd leadership of Marshal Mikhail Kutuzov assembled near the town of Olmütz about 100 miles (160 km) to the north. As on many other occasions in his military career Napoleon had seemingly placed himself in a trap.

All the allies had to do was wait. Napoleon's army was exposed and would only get weaker. Allied reinforcements were on the way from Austrian units in Italy and from Russia. But the Russian emperor, Czar Alexander I, believing victory was in sight, overruled Kutuzov. He ordered an attack. The result was the Battle of Austerlitz on December 2, 1805, a major French victory. Two days later the Austrians surrendered and the Russians retreated.

The treaty that Napoleon made with the Austrians gave him complete control of their former areas of influence in Germany and Italy. Napoleon spent the first half of 1806 organizing these territories into French-controlled puppet states ready to serve his interests and send him troops. Prussia's leaders made the unwise decision that with Austria out of the war and Russia too far away to help that this was the right time to fight France.

War with Prussia

Napoleon's army was massed in southern Germany. His forces were now routinely divided up into miniature armies called corps. Each of these was usually commanded by one of the emperor's trusted marshals and was normally 20,000 to 30,000 men strong. Each corps had infantry, cavalry, and artillery of its own, and so was capable of independent operations or of fighting as part of a larger battle plan.

On October 8, 1806, Napoleon invaded Prussia's ally Saxony (in southeastern Germany) in what was his standard formation with the various army corps spread well apart. This formation

At Austerlitz Napoleon deliberately made his right flank weak. The allies believed they could crush it and surround him. But General Louis Davout secretly led his forces from Vienna to reinforce the right flank. While the allies were bogged down fighting Davout, Napoleon unleashed a decisive attack in the center.

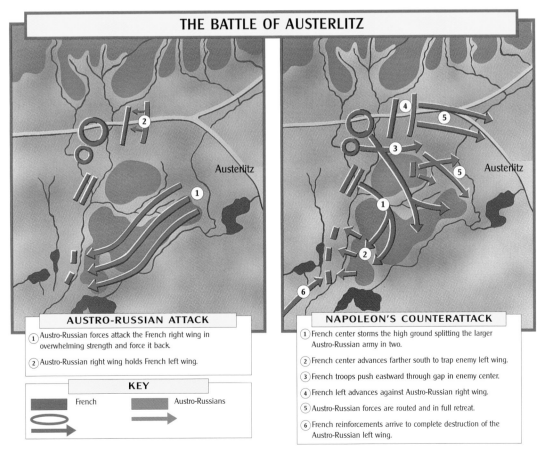

THE BATTLE OF AUSTERLITZ

AUSTRO-RUSSIAN ATTACK

1. Austro-Russian forces attack the French right wing in overwhelming strength and force it back.
2. Austro-Russian right wing holds French left wing.

KEY

| | French | | Austro-Russians |

NAPOLEON'S COUNTERATTACK

1. French center storms the high ground splitting the larger Austro-Russian army in two.
2. French center advances farther south to trap enemy left wing.
3. French troops push eastward through gap in enemy center.
4. French left advances against Austro-Russian right wing.
5. Austro-Russian forces are routed and in full retreat.
6. French reinforcements arrive to complete destruction of the Austro-Russian left wing.

helped the French troops advance quickly, but at the same time they were close enough to each other to unite. The ability to suddenly concentrate his forces was one of Napoleon's greatest skills.

It only took Napoleon six days to win the victory he wanted, but it did not all go according to plan. Napoleon concentrated 90,000 men at Jena in eastern Germany on October 14 and

LOUIS NICOLAS DAVOUT

Marshal Davout was the most successful of Napoleon's commanders. From 1805 until Napoleon's final defeat Davout was always given a key role, usually commanding one of the semi-independent army corps that made up Napoleon's Grand Army. Davout never lost a battle.

Napoleon gave Davout the title Duke of Auerstadt when his skill and great determination had saved his corps in the fighting in 1806. In 1809 Davout acquired another title, Prince of Eckmühl, following an equally impressive victory in a preliminary battle against the Austrians that year. But Davout and his men also performed vital roles at the great victories of Austerlitz and Wagram, and at many other battles.

In the Russian campaign of 1812, and the fighting between 1813 and 1814, when Napoleon was gradually pushed back into France, Davout remained loyal and did more than any of the other marshals to delay the inevitable defeat.

When Napoleon returned to power in 1815 he left Davout in Paris running the home army as minister of war because there was no one else he trusted as much. Some historians think Davout was such a good general that Napoleon would have won the Battle of Waterloo, if he had had Davout with him.

Napoleon salutes his troops as they go into action at Auerstadt, the battle at which Davout earned the title of duke.

Austrian generals and their staff officers survey the Battle of Aspern-Essling, fought over two days in May 1809. The battle was Napoleon's first defeat. France had about 25,000 men killed or wounded during the fight.

defeated what he thought was the main Prussian force, but in fact it was only a part, some 40,000 men. At the same time about 15 miles (24 km) away at Auerstadt, Marshal Louis Davout's 27,000 troops were fighting for their lives and winning against 50,000 more Prussians. Napoleon could now have made peace but he decided he could do better by continuing to attack Russia.

By the end of the year Napoleon had moved his army into what is now Poland. The Battle of Eylau on February 8, 1807, was confused and bloody, fought in the middle of a heavy snowstorm. The Russians and French both had to retreat. Napoleon told the French people that he had won another victory, but with one third of his army dead or wounded this was a lie.

Europe-wide war

Napoleon got the victory he was looking for when fighting resumed in the summer. The Russian commander, Count Lévin Bennigsen, positioned his army badly so that its various sections could not support each other properly. The Russians lost about 25,000 casualties in the Battle of Friedland in eastern Poland on June 14, three times as many as the French. A few weeks later Napoleon agreed to the Treaty of Tilsit with Russia and Prussia.

After a brief campaign in Spain in 1808 Napoleon was caught off guard by the Austrians who attacked unexpectedly in 1809. He suffered his first defeat at the Battle of Aspern-Essling east of

Vienna on May 21–22. He had to bring up reinforcements. This time he made careful plans and preparations before going into battle. Napoleon won the Battle of Wagram, fought on July 5–6.

Wagram was a huge battle, with Napoleon's 185,000 troops facing 155,000 Austrians commanded by the Archduke Charles. The two sides pounded at each other brutally for the two days of fighting. There was little clever maneuvering. The decisive moment came on the second day. Napoleon had been trying to smash the Austrian army's left wing, but had met with stiff opposition on the first day.

On the second day he concentrated his artillery against the Austrian center and then launched a huge infantry attack. The attack pushed through the Austrian line and was supported by a renewed onslaught against the Austrian left wing. In the end the Austrians, hammered by Napoleon's twin-pronged attack, had to retreat. They had about 40,000 casualties; the French around 35,000. Austria had to make peace and gave up more territory.

A unit of the French Imperial Guard (right) repulses an attack by enemy cavalry during the Battle of Aspern-Essling in May 1809.

COLUMN VERSUS LINE

Most of the troops in the armies of the Napoleonic Wars were infantry foot soldiers. In battle they usually fought close together, side by side with their comrades. They also usually fought in one of two formations, either line or column.

When they fought in line, an infantry battalion of 600 or 800 men would stand in two or three ranks with each rank therefore anything up to 400 men wide. This gave every man in the unit a chance to fire his musket without his friends getting in the way. But it took a lot of training for men to use their muskets properly and even more drill for them to learn to maneuver when spread out like this. Line was usually the best formation for defense but did not work as well as a column in attack.

Columns were better formations for maneuver and sometimes for attacks. A battalion column might have 50 or 60 men in the front rank and be about 12 ranks deep.

Soldiers in a column did not have to worry about keeping their lines straight and so could concentrate on moving quickly. Men in the middle of a column would not be able to use their weapons but often their speed and the fear of what attacking columns might do was enough to make their enemies pull back.

Napoleon's lust for power had gotten him into trouble once again and his careless military preparations had made things worse at the start. Again, as in Italy in 1797, or at Austerlitz in 1805, or at Friedland in 1807, Napoleon had saved himself with a great victory, this time at Wagram, and then persuaded his enemies to make peace on his terms. However, Napoleon's army had huge casualties at Wagram, including many veterans.

Victory but no peace

Napoleon had won all of these victories between 1805 and 1809 partly due to his own brilliant leadership but also partly thanks to the fighting skills of his generals and their veteran French troops. Now his veterans were becoming more and more worn out by almost constant warfare and his army was increasingly made up of untrained conscripts and unreliable units drawn from France's German or Italian puppet states. Napoleon was master of the whole of Western and Central Europe, but if he failed to win his next big battle, he would be in trouble once more. He faced two challenges—from a continuing war in Spain and from Russia, which was allied with Britain.

Napoleonic Naval Warfare

During the Revolutionary and Napoleonic Wars Britain's power and wealth were based on maritime trade. To protect this and keep Britain safe from invasion, the British had maintained the world's strongest navy for many years. Throughout the war years from 1792 to 1815 Britain used its trading wealth not only to finance wars but also to pay other countries if they were willing to fight against France. The British navy was at the height of its power and stopped any attempts to undermine the country's economic power.

France tried to strike back at Britain's economic power in two ways. Up to the Battle of Trafalgar, off the southwest coast of Spain in 1805, France tried to attack Britain at sea and by threatening invasion. All these attempts failed. In 1806 Napoleon introduced the Continental System. With this he forced other European countries to agree not to import British goods, aiming to destroy Britain's economy and force it to make peace.

Vital naval power
Unfortunately for Napoleon his reluctant European partners never shut out enough of Britain's trade for this system to work either. Although there were no large naval battles in the last ten years of the war, naval power was vital in defeating Napoleon.

The British fleet bombards the Danish capital, Copenhagen, in September 1807. The British launched this attack to prevent Denmark and Russia from joining a European alliance with France. The attack was successful and the Danish fleet surrendered.

All the naval vessels used in the Napoleonic Wars were sail- or, rarely, oar-powered. The first steamships were coming into service but none was used for military purposes. Battleships in the major navies, known as ships-of-the-line, were manned by between 600 and 1,000 men and carried from 70 to over 100 cannon, mounted along the sides of the ships on several decks. If they got close to an enemy these could fire smashing broadsides, battering an enemy ship to pieces and killing many of its crew.

Ships were always subject to the wind and weather. Movement at sea could never be predictable in the way that a land army could be relied on to march a number of miles in its chosen direction each day. Life at sea was always dangerous—far more ships were sunk by bad weather or navigational mistakes than were ever lost due to enemy action.

Experience and hard practice

On the other hand sailing ships obviously never needed to refuel. Moreover, the ships could carry enough food and other supplies to stay at sea for weeks or even months at a time if their crews were skilled and experienced enough. Warships were in fact the most complicated machines in existence and years of experience and hard practice were needed to command a ship or maneuver a fleet.

Throughout the wars Britain's strategy was based on blockade. This meant that British fleets always patrolled close to enemy ports, keeping enemy trading vessels and warships imprisoned. They also practiced ship-handling and maneuvering at the same time. France started the wars with the problem of having lost many experienced naval officers (most were aristocrats) because of the Revolution. The British blockade meant that the French never spent enough time at sea to become as effective as

---

BRITISH NAVAL TACTICS

Because of the common problems of maneuvering clumsy sailing battleships, and because of cautious tactics, naval battles were often indecisive in the 18th century. The British navy had its own drill book called the *Permanent Fighting Instructions*, which laid down exactly what captains and admirals should do in battle.

Unfortunately, doing things by the book tended to take so long that the enemy could slip away. In the Napoleonic Wars the best British commanders were prepared to disobey these instructions if it gave them a chance to close in on the enemy and destroy them.

At the Battle of Cape St. Vincent, at the southwestern end of Portugal, in 1797, when Horatio Nelson was a commodore, he took his ship out of the line of battle to cut off the Spanish escape. If he had failed, he could have been executed for disobeying orders. Instead he made the British victory possible and blocked the Franco-Spanish plan to unite their fleets to cover an invasion of Britain.

The flagship of the French admiral at the Battle of the Nile in August 1798 is devastated by an internal explosion after being pounded by the British under Nelson. This one-sided battle ended with the destruction of all but three of 13 French warships. Nelson's victory ended Napoleon's attempt to take over Egypt.

before. British sailors and their commanders were much better trained. Despite these advantages it took much hard fighting before the British completely took control. The years of greatest crises were from 1796 to 1798 and 1805.

In the first years of the war Holland and Spain had been Britain's allies but French victories on land made them decide to switch sides. British resources were stretched so thin that Britain pulled its fleet out of the Mediterranean in 1796, abandoning its allies and trading interests there. Late in 1796 the French tried to invade British-controlled Ireland. A poor British commander did not do much to stop them but the expedition failed because of terrible weather.

An even worse crisis for the British followed in April 1797, when most of their home-based fleets mutinied. Almost all the crews refused to obey orders in protest at the poor food they were given, their late pay, and harsh discipline. Some of the mutineers' demands were agreed to and the mutiny ended but until August that year Britain was practically undefended.

British victories

Away from home waters the British fleets were not affected by the mutiny because their commanders took better care of their men. The Royal Navy began to regain the initiative when Admiral John Jervis defeated a Spanish fleet in the Battle of Cape St. Vincent off southwest Portugal on February 14, 1797. In October the home fleet proved that it could be relied on again when it destroyed the Dutch fleet at the Battle of Camperdown in Holland on the North Sea. The next year Jervis sent part of his force back into the Mediterranean. Led by Admiral Horatio Nelson this squadron went on to annihilate the French Mediterranean fleet in the Battle of the Nile on August 1.

When war between Britain and France resumed in 1803 after the brief Peace of Amiens, Britain's enemies had rebuilt their fleets and were ready to try again. Napoleon assembled his "Army of England" along France's northern coast. If the British navy could be kept from interfering while he transported his army across the narrow waters of the English Channel there was no doubt that he could easily conquer Britain. Instead his elaborate plan finally fell apart with the crushing British victory at Trafalgar.

British naval power was vital to the defeat of Napoleon. Napoleon's invasion of Russia in 1812 was caused by Russia trading with Britain despite Napoleon's attempts to isolate Britain from Europe. British warships protected the trade with Russia and there was no French fleet to stop it. A land campaign was the only way Napoleon could break the trading links.

THE BATTLE OF TRAFALGAR

The Battle of Trafalgar off the southwest coast of Spain on October 21, 1805, began when Napoleon tried to bring the French and Spanish fleets together to support an invasion of Britain. He ordered the French fleet under Admiral Pierre de Villeneuve and various Spanish detachments to a rendezvous in the Caribbean.

The French plan was to draw the British navy away from the English Channel, thereby allowing the invasion army to land without hindrance. Nelson led his squadron after them across the Atlantic but did not catch them. When he realized the French plan, he returned to join the British fleet in the English Channel. He learned that Villeneuve had sailed back to the Spanish port of Cadiz. Napoleon ordered Villeneuve to sail from Cadiz to the French port of Brest but by then Nelson was waiting.

Villeneuve had 18 French and 15 Spanish ships. Nelson was outnumbered but he was so confident of the superior seamanship of his men that he steered into the enemy. Nelson himself was killed in the battle that followed but 18 of the enemy ships were captured or sunk.

The French warship Redoubtable, *its mast and rigging shot away by very close-range cannon fire, continues to slug it out with a British vessel at Trafalgar.*

NAPOLEON'S "SPANISH ULCER"

The war in Spain and Portugal, also known as the Peninsular War, began as a minor operation but it soon became Napoleon's "Spanish Ulcer." It was a war that painfully drained away the strength of his armies and finally helped to ruin his empire. Spain was France's ally in 1807 and was supposedly taking part in Napoleon's anti-British trade embargo, the Continental System. Portugal was a neutral country. It imported British goods for its own use and sent them on into Spain. Napoleon was determined to put a stop to this.

With Spanish permission Napoleon sent a small army across Spain and into Portugal toward the end of 1807. Napoleon also decided to depose the Spanish king and replace him with someone he could trust to apply the Continental System effectively.

The new Spanish king was to be Napoleon's brother, Joseph, and another army was sent off to Spain to put Joseph securely in charge. The Spanish people were furious and began a rebellion against the French in May 1808. A French force of 20,000 troops was even surrounded and forced to surrender at Baylen in July.

These events gave Britain an opportunity to intervene. Britain sent an expedition to help the Portuguese. A young British general called Arthur Wellesley defeated the French at the Battle of

The war in Spain was characterized by atrocities on all sides. This painting by Spanish artist Francisco de Goya shows citizens of Madrid being executed by French troops on May 3, 1808, after a rebellion against the invaders.

WELLINGTON'S WAY OF WAR

Arthur Wellesley, the Duke of Wellington, was the British commander-in-chief in Spain from the summer of 1809 until the end of the Napoleonic Wars. He led the British forces in the final decisive victory over Napoleon at Waterloo in 1815.

Napoleon's forces won many of their successes throughout his long wars by concentrating on fast maneuvering and aggressive attacks. Wellington's victories were based on different methods. He always made sure his armies were properly supplied. In battle he relied on the firepower of his infantry to smash the enemy maneuvers rather than trying to beat them at their own game.

Wellington tried to make the enemy do most of the attacking in his battles, while he kept his men hidden behind the crests of hills. This protected them from the French artillery. Then, when the French advanced, his infantry were ready to shoot them down with volleys of close-range musket fire.

Vimeiro in August 1808 and the French commander agreed to leave Portugal. This was the last straw for Napoleon. He took his main army to Spain to solve the problem himself.

By the end of October 1808 Napoleon had 200,000 men massed in northern Spain. Within six weeks he had smashed the Spanish armies and captured the capital city, Madrid. He planned to finish the job by launching offensives into southern Spain and Portugal. He was unable to do so because British troops commanded by General Sir John Moore had attacked his line of communications to the north. Napoleon sent his armies north.

Spain fights back

Moore's forces made a desperate retreat and were evacuated by sea from La Coruña, but they had prevented Napoleon from carrying out his original plan. Napoleon left Spain, never to return in person, to fight bigger battles in Austria. His generals were left to complete the victory but it was a far harder task than their emperor anticipated. The Spanish forces fought on and the British built up their base in Portugal to help them.

Napoleon never realized how different from the rest of Europe Spain was. Spain was a poor country with scarcely enough food for its own people, never mind an additional 200,000 or more French troops. Even so the French forces were ordered to live largely off the land.

The war in Spain and Portugal lasted from 1807 to 1812. Napoleon was eventually defeated, in part because he was unwilling to devote the time and resources to defeat the alliance of British, Spanish, and Portuguese armies arrayed against him.

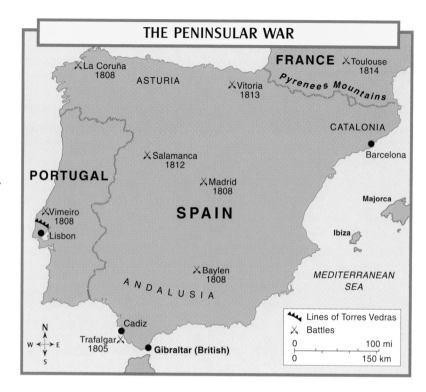

THE PENINSULAR WAR

FRANCE
× Toulouse 1814

× La Coruña 1808
ASTURIA
× Vitoria 1813
Pyrenees Mountains

CATALONIA

× Salamanca 1812
Barcelona

PORTUGAL
× Madrid 1808

Majorca

× Vimeiro 1808
SPAIN

Lisbon
Ibiza

× Baylen 1808
MEDITERRANEAN SEA

ANDALUSIA

N
W ← → E
S

Cadiz
Trafalgar × 1805
Gibraltar (British)

Lines of Torres Vedras
× Battles
0   100 mi
0   150 km

The Spanish armies never won a significant battle after Baylen, but they kept trying. Even worse for the French was the guerrilla struggle. Tens of thousands of French troops had to be used to protect their communications. Whenever French soldiers stole food from the Spanish, as they had to do if they wanted to eat, they turned more and more Spaniards into guerrilla fighters.

The Duke of Wellington

The fighting in Spain divides up into two phases. Between 1809 and 1811 the French were the stronger, aiming to expel the British from Portugal. From 1812 until the end of the war in the spring of 1814, the British were on the attack, conquering the French armies and advancing into southern France.

Throughout both periods the British were inspired by the careful but effective leadership of General Arthur Wellesley whose victories gained him the title of Duke of Wellington. Wellington sometimes had to retreat but he never lost a battle in either phase of the war. In the earlier period he attacked the French whenever he could, but knew he would usually have to fall back to Portugal if the French concentrated their forces.

He made sure, however, that his base around Lisbon was fortified by the defensive positions known as the Lines of Torres Vedras. In 1810, when Wellington was forced to retreat to this base, the French army that followed him virtually starved while Wellington's men had supplies brought in by British ships.

The British forces were stronger by 1812 and the French could expect fewer reinforcements from home with Napoleon heading for disaster in Russia. Wellington smashed a French force at the Battle of Salamanca on July 12, 1812, but had to retreat later in the year after an over-ambitious offensive failed.

A drain on resources

Wellington made no mistake in 1813. King Joseph's army was virtually destroyed in the Battle of Vitoria on June 21. Other French forces had no option but to pull out of Spain entirely. By early 1814 Wellington was in southern France. The British captured the city of Toulouse on April 10, where they learned that Napoleon had abdicated his throne and the war was over.

Napoleon always thought that Spain was a minor war theater, but it turned into a relentless drain on France's resources. The Peninsular War proved to the rest of Europe that Britain would help its allies and keep on fighting as long as was necessary. It also proved that France's armies could be beaten.

British infantry (in red coats) launch the final attack in their victory over the French at Vitoria in 1813. The Duke of Wellington (left, with telescope) looks on.

THE 1812 RUSSIAN CAMPAIGN

Russia and France became allies of a sort when they agreed to the Treaty of Tilsit in 1807, but relations between the two soon began to deteriorate. There were various quarrels between them, especially over the French trade embargo against Britain, the Continental System. By the summer of 1811 Napoleon had decided that he was going to have a showdown with the Russians. He began to prepare in earnest for war toward the end of that year. By 1812 Napoleon had a huge army ready to invade Russia.

Napoleon (third from right) meets Emperor Alexander I (left) of Russia on a raft on the Niemen River to discuss the Treaty of Tilsit in 1807. Alexander and Frederick William III of Prussia, their armies recently smashed by Napoleon, had to accept humiliating peace terms.

Napoleon set about mobilizing his largest army yet, about 600,000 men. About 450,000 of these would actually advance into Russia, the remainder would protect the main army's flanks. Napoleon also ordered special preparations to be made for the unusual conditions that his troops would meet. Russia was poorer and a lot more backward than most other parts of Europe. Napoleon's men could not expect to be able to live off the land to the extent that they might in Germany or Italy.

Napoleon plunges into Russia

Russia was also a huge country. Napoleon's army would have to march over 500 miles (800 km) to Moscow from the French-controlled state, the Duchy of Warsaw, which was Napoleon's forward base. Supplies and replacements would have to come from France, several hundred miles farther west of the duchy.

Napoleon made all the right moves in preparing to meet these problems. He gave orders for huge quantities of rations and other supplies to be assembled, along with all the carts and animals needed to pull them. The factories and supply officers were only able to provide a small part of what Napoleon wanted, but this did not make him change his plans.

THE GRAND ARMY

After Napoleon made himself emperor of France in 1804, he normally called his main army the Grand Army. The Grand Army that he put together for the invasion of Russia in 1812 was the biggest yet but it was not necessarily the best.

The main force, which he commanded himself, was about 250,000 strong and included most of his best troops and top generals. One of his brothers and his stepson each commanded flanking units of about 75,000 men.

About 30,000 Prussian allies operated separately to the north and the same number of Austrians to the south. Together with the second line forces this made a total of close to 600,000 men available to serve with Napoleon.

Altogether there were about 12 nationalities involved, for Napoleon had recruited troops from all the French-controlled German and Italian states. Only about half were Frenchmen. Only they and the Polish troops could really be relied on.

It was the biggest army the world had ever seen but within six months it had collapsed, suffering over 300,000 casualties. Most died from disease, starvation, exhaustion, and cold, rather than in battle.

The advance and retreat of Napoleon's Grand Army during the 1812 Russian campaign. Napoleon was forced to retreat from Moscow and eventually abandoned his men to their fate.

Napoleon ordered his men to cross the Niemen River into Russia late on June 23, 1812. As usual he planned to fight a decisive battle as soon as possible and then dictate peace terms. Instead the Russians retreated, having first destroyed any useful supplies the French might capture. By mid-August Napoleon had advanced to Smolensk. He tried three times to catch parts of the retreating Russian armies, but the Russians escaped each time.

The main part of Napoleon's army had been about 250,000 strong when it crossed into Russia but was now down to less than 160,000 because of disease, starvation, and general exhaustion. Napoleon halted for a week to rest and decide what to do next. On August 24 he ordered an advance once again, still convinced that winning a battle would solve all his problems.

The Battle of Borodino

The Russians now appointed a new commander-in-chief. General Mikhail Kutuzov was nearly 70 years old, but he was still tough and cunning. His favorite strategy was always to wear an enemy down gradually. If he had to fight, he made sure he chose his position well. Kutuzov ordered his men to dig in near a village called Borodino, about 70 miles (112 km) west of Moscow.

The two sides both had about 130,000 men but the Russians had slightly more artillery. Kutuzov's position was protected by a river, a number of ravines, and woods on one flank. The Russian artillery and part of the infantry were dug in on top of a series of hills. Some of Napoleon's officers wanted to maneuver around behind the Russian defenses. Napoleon said this would only give Kutuzov another chance to slip away and avoid battle. Napoleon needed a decisive victory.

The only alternative plan for the French was a frontal attack. The battle was fought on September 7 and turned into a brutal slogging match. The French attacks pushed slowly forward with fierce charges and artillery bombardments causing huge casualties to both sides. By nightfall the French had captured the Russian defenses, but both sides were too exhausted to fight any more. French casualties were over 30,000 men; the Russians suffered about 40,000 casualties.

On to Moscow

Kutuzov retreated the next day, but it was not the victory that Napoleon wanted. On September 14 the French moved into Moscow and got two unwelcome surprises. Most of the people had left and over the next few days much of the city burned to the ground in huge fires started on Russian orders. There would be no shelter and little food in Moscow for Napoleon's army, with the Russian winter fast approaching.

The major battle of the 1812 campaign was fought at Borodino on September 7, 1812. Napoleon opted to attack but his plans were not clever enough. His troops launched frontal assaults against the Russians, many of whom were behind fortifications (as here). Losses on both sides were very heavy.

THE COSSACKS

In Russian history the cossacks originated as bands of outlaws on the steppes (grasslands). The name cossack is taken from a Turkish word that means vagabond. Cossack bands on horseback also worked as mercenaries. By the Napoleonic Wars they made up a large part of the light cavalry force of the Russian army.

Cossack troops were not usually very effective fighters in battle but they excelled at harassing enemy forces in skirmishes or launching hit-and-run attacks. They were also experts when it came to coping with the snow and extreme cold of the Russian winter.

During the 1812 campaign they played a vital role in wearing the French down. About 15,000 cossacks fought in 1812. Cossacks captured messengers, killed stragglers, blocked supply convoys, and generally made sure that Napoleon's men were exhausted by being constantly on the alert. During the retreat from Moscow Napoleon himself was nearly captured by a cossack charge.

Throughout the French retreat the cossacks were always nearby, helping create the atmosphere of fear that turned the retreating Grand Army into a demoralized rabble.

Napoleon had another bout of wishful thinking. He had won a battle and captured the most important city in the enemy country, so surely they would make peace, just as they always had in the past? Napoleon delayed for a month before he realized that the Russians would not give up. The retreat from Moscow began on October 19. Napoleon's army was now down to 95,000 men.

The retreat begins

Napoleon still hoped to inflict a defeat on the Russians as he fell back from Moscow. He led the Grand Army south from the capital and came up against Kutuzov's army at Maloyaroslavets on October 24. The drawn battle there was not the victory that Napoleon needed. He decided to head north toward Borodino and then retreat westward following the same route he had used just a few months before during his advance on Moscow.

By November 12 the French were back in Smolensk, where what was left of their supply system broke down completely. Their numbers were down to about 50,000 men because of Russian raids and skirmishes, exhaustion, and lack of food. Horses were killed for their flesh and there were incidents of cannibalism. The cold and snows of winter had also begun.

The Russians were snapping at the heels of the disintegrating Grand Army. Part of Kutuzov's army got behind the French and blocked their line of retreat at Krasnoi on November 16–17. The French cut through the Russians but suffered heavy casualties. At the end of November the French had to get across one of the rivers blocking their route, the Berezina. A few bridges were thrown across the icy river, but Russian artillery fire caused panic. Discipline was lost as men crowded across the only escape routes.

Napoleon leaves his army behind

When the French destroyed the bridges at dawn, thousands of soldiers were left trapped on the Russian side of the Berezina. After the Battle of the Berezina the Russians said that they counted 13,000 frozen corpses. Only about 20,000 French troops finally escaped, ragged, starving, and frostbitten. They were no more than a disorganized mob and not an army any more.

Napoleon left his troops behind in Poland and hurried back to France. He knew that some of his allies would now desert him and join the British and the Russians. Napoleon still thought his military genius would get him out of the mess. He put the catastrophe of the Russian campaign behind him and set to work organizing new armies for the battles that were to come.

The remnants of the Grand Army struggle to cross the Berezina River in November 1812. Men panicked and many were thrown into the icy waters where they drowned or succumbed to the extreme cold.

NAPOLEON IN RETREAT

The year 1813 began with more bad news for Napoleon. Austria became neutral, giving up its unwilling alliance with France. Then the Prussians began negotiations with the Russians. Prussia declared war on France in March, forming yet another anti-French coalition with Russia, Sweden, and Britain. With the enemy alliance advancing in strength toward the French borders, Napoleon was facing the greatest test of his military abilities that he had ever faced. He would fight well but be forced to surrender in April 1814.

By the spring of 1813 the Russians and their new allies had freed the whole of Poland and the eastern half of Germany. Napoleon's forces retreated west of the Elbe River. The Russian forces had suffered almost as badly as Napoleon's in the fighting of 1812, and they and their new allies had become strung out by their advance. They had only about 100,000 men with their forward units, though reinforcements were on the way. Napoleon decided to attack with his as yet untried troops.

Heavy French losses

The first battle was at Lützen in eastern Germany on May 2. Because his cavalry scouts were so weak, part of Napoleon's army was caught by surprise. Napoleon brought up reinforcements just

French, Russian, and Prussian troops clash at the Battle of Bautzen in May 1813. Napoleon came close to destroying the forces arrayed against him, but one of his generals failed to carry out the flanking maneuver that would have trapped the enemy army.

THE 1813 CAMPAIGN

BALTIC SEA

Tilsit

Danzig

PRUSSIA

RUSSIA

Elbe River

RHINE

Berlin

**GRAND DUCHY
OF
WARSAW**

Warsaw

CONFEDERATION OF THE
(GERMANY)

Bautzen

Oder River

Leipzig

Breslau

Lützen

Dresden

Prague

AUSTRIA

Battles

0   100 mi

0   150 km

Despite the loss of the Grand Army in 1812, Napoleon was able to rebuild his forces but many of his soldiers were raw recruits. Napoleon hoped to defeat the armies of those countries allied against him in 1813 one by one. If they combined their much larger forces, he would have little chance of winning the war. His allies did combine against him at the Battle of Leipzig in October and Napoleon suffered very heavy losses.

in time, leading some of the attacks himself. It was enough to win the battle and make the enemy pull back. But each side suffered about 20,000 casualties, making it the sort of victory that Napoleon with his dwindling reserves of manpower could not afford to repeat.

The armies fought again at Bautzen on May 20–21, and the result was very much the same. The French victory at Bautzen remained incomplete, with again about 20,000 casualties suffered by Napoleon's forces. Both sides were now very tired and disorganized. They agreed to halt fighting for the moment, supposedly to let their diplomats patch up some sort of peace agreement between them.

Napoleon's enemies close in

In fact both sides used the delay to build up their forces once more. This process did the allies far more good than the French. The crucial point came on August 12, when Austria declared war on France. Europe had been at war with France for 20 years but this was the first time that four major nations—Russia, Prussia, Austria, and Britain—fought France at the same time.

Fighting began again immediately after the Austrian decision to go to war. The allies had a new strategy. They would try to attack parts of the French army, but whenever Napoleon himself arrived with his reserves they would pull back. The French reserves would be worn out by rushing from place to place.

Napoleon did win a major victory at Dresden on August 26–27, when his 120,000 men caught an Austrian-led force of 170,000. The Austrians had about 35,000 casualties to the French 10,000, but the remainder of their army managed to retreat, ready to fight another day. Unfortunately for Napoleon there were four other substantial battles during that August and September. In each, one of his generals was defeated.

The decisive battle finally came at Leipzig in Germany on October 16–19, 1813. The French were outnumbered by the allied armies and badly beaten. By the start of November the French had retreated west of the Rhine River. Napoleon had built his forces up to about 450,000 men in the course of the year. Now he had only 70,000 left, plus stragglers and various garrisons cut off in Germany.

Napoleon assembled about 100,000 troops to protect France from invasion, but after he had manned various fortresses his field army consisted of about 40,000 men. They faced three advancing allied forces of well over 300,000 men in all. However,

THE BATTLE OF LEIPZIG

The Battle of Leipzig in October 1813 was probably the largest battle that had ever been fought to that date. Because so many different countries' armies took part in the fighting, it became known as the "Battle of the Nations."

Four allied armies and the French forces closed in on Leipzig from both the north and the south in October. Only two of the allied armies arrived in time for the first day of the battle on October 16. The fighting was indecisive with about 30,000 casualties on each side.

There was little fighting on the 17th but the battlefront roared into life again on the 18th and 19th. Napoleon was now badly outnumbered by about 365,000 troops to 190,000. The French had to retreat. It was not easy because there was only one bridge over the Elster River. The bridge had been prepared for demolition. Suddenly the soldier in charge panicked and blew it up. Over 30,000 French troops were stranded on the wrong side and were captured. It turned a defeat for Napoleon into a disaster.

NAPOLEON ABDICATES

Even though it was foolhardy for Napoleon to try to fight on in 1814, rather than make peace, his maneuvers in January and February showed some of the best generalship of his military career.

A crucial difference was that all the armies were very much smaller after the fierce fighting of the recent months. Napoleon always tried to control everything that his armies did himself. This simply was not possible with the huge forces he had used in his later years and was part of the reason why things had gone wrong for him. Now, with only 40,000 men he could coordinate his forces properly once again.

One allied army was invading France from the northeast and another from the east. Napoleon decided to move between them to keep them apart and then fight them one at a time. For most of January and February Napoleon was able to keep his enemies off balance but in the end it was all a waste of lives and effort. Napoleon was forced to abdicate in April 1814.

Napoleon bids farewell to his Imperial Guard shortly after his abdication on April 11, 1814.

Napoleon was not daunted by the odds he faced and decided to attack. Despite his worsening health, he showed some of his old brilliance and frequently outmaneuvered his enemies. The French won a series of battles in northeast France in January and February 1814. The allied leaders almost panicked in the face of these unexpected defeats, but recovered their nerve. Their armies advanced again, closing in on Paris.

Napoleon goes into exile

At the end of March the allies reached Paris. Napoleon's generals told him to give up. Leading French politicians invited a member of the pre-1789 French royal family to rule France as Louis XVIII. On April 11, 1814, Napoleon abdicated. He was sent into exile on Elba, a small island in the Mediterranean off the Italian coast. It seemed that the Napoleonic Wars were over.

The Hundred Days Campaign

After his defeat in 1814 Napoleon stayed in exile on the tiny Italian island of Elba for less than a year. His ambition and his belief in his own destiny were as strong as ever. He knew that many people in France were unhappy with the government of King Louis XVIII. He also knew that the victorious European powers might not be able to unite against him yet again. Napoleon left Elba on February 26, 1815, and sailed for France. His hopes of regaining his throne would last just one hundred days—until his defeat at Waterloo.

Napoleon sailed back to France with the 1,000 men of his personal guard. These troops made up the only army he had left. His march through France quickly became a triumphant parade, however. Thousands of old soldiers flocked to support their emperor. The French royal family fled and on March 20 Napoleon entered Paris as emperor once more.

After he had sent troops to guard France's borders, Napoleon had about 125,000 men left to use in his planned offensive. It was a top-quality army, packed with tough veterans. This fighting power meant that Napoleon could beat either of his British and

General Count von Gneisenau (pointing) gives orders to his staff officers during the Battle of Ligny on June 16, 1815. The Prussians were defeated by the French but were able to retreat in good order. Two days later they would link up with the British at Waterloo to defeat Napoleon's army.

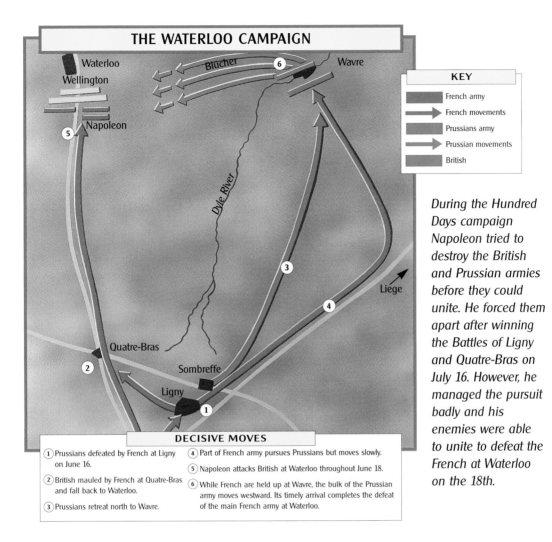

THE WATERLOO CAMPAIGN

KEY

- French army
- French movements
- Prussians army
- Prussian movements
- British

DECISIVE MOVES

1. Prussians defeated by French at Ligny on June 16.

2. British mauled by French at Quatre-Bras and fall back to Waterloo.

3. Prussians retreat north to Wavre.

4. Part of French army pursues Prussians but moves slowly.

5. Napoleon attacks British at Waterloo throughout June 18.

6. While French are held up at Wavre, the bulk of the Prussian army moves westward. Its timely arrival completes the defeat of the main French army at Waterloo.

During the Hundred Days campaign Napoleon tried to destroy the British and Prussian armies before they could unite. He forced them apart after winning the Battles of Ligny and Quatre-Bras on July 16. However, he managed the pursuit badly and his enemies were able to unite to defeat the French at Waterloo on the 18th.

Prussian opponents separately. If they managed to work together properly, there were so many of them that Napoleon could not win. Napoleon's strategy was to drive between the two enemy armies to push them apart and then beat them one at a time.

The French attack

Napoleon assembled his army in northern France. His first moves against his enemies on June 15 were unexpected. The Duke of Wellington had ordered his army to concentrate in the wrong location, too far west of his Prussian allies under Field Marshal Gebhard von Blücher. Blücher set about assembling his forces but many of them would not arrive in time to fight the next day.

SQUARE VERSUS CAVALRY

Some of the most desperate French attacks at Waterloo were carried out by their cavalry. Cavalry could destroy an infantry unit if they caught it in the open in the usual infantry formations of line or column. When infantrymen were menaced by cavalry, they had no option but to use another formation known as the square.

Infantry in a square faced in all four directions. Some men would kneel and some would stand but all would point their muskets and bayonets outward. Cavalry could not charge into a properly formed square but a square could not move or do very much else. Squares were sitting ducks for a close-range artillery bombardment.

The French cavalry attacks at Waterloo succeeded in getting among the allied infantry battalions and forcing them into the square formation. If Napoleon's generals had brought their artillery forward quickly enough to smash the squares, they might have won the battle.

Two separate battles were fought on June 16. Wellington's advance guard was heavily outnumbered at first at Quatre-Bras, but the French dithered and were slow to attack. Each time the French seemed about to break through, just enough British reinforcements arrived to hold on. By the end of the day Quatre-Bras was still in British hands and Wellington had gotten his army back together again, without being punished too badly for his mistake of the day before.

Blücher, however, had been defeated. His 83,000 Prussians fought 77,000 French under Napoleon's personal command at the Battle of Ligny (known in France as the Battle of Fleurus). There was fierce fighting throughout the afternoon and evening but given the quality of the two armies there could only be one result. Despite its heavy casualties the Prussian army was not destroyed, however. The Prussians retreated in good order and would recover to fight again.

Pointless marching

One vital mistake prevented the day from becoming another French triumph. About 20,000 French troops did not fire a shot. It would not even have mattered which battle they fought in. Because of a mix-up in their orders, they marched backward and forward between the two battles and achieved nothing.

A second French mistake now followed. Napoleon thought that Blücher's men had retreated eastward, completely losing touch with the British. In fact they had gone north, with Blücher still determined to support Wellington if he possibly could.

Wellington had to retreat from Quatre-Bras, but with Blücher's promise of support he decided to make a stand near Waterloo on June 18. Wellington had about 68,000 men by this time and Napoleon about 72,000. The rest of Napoleon's army, about 30,000 troops under Marshal Emmanuel de Grouchy, was off trying to chase Blücher's Prussians, but they were heading in the wrong direction. In fact most of Blücher's army was bearing down on the French right flank at Waterloo.

Napoleon still had time to win the battle against Wellington before the Prussians arrived but instead he allowed his officers to make a series of poorly-planned attacks. These were blocked by Wellington. All the time more and more of the French troops were being drawn into the fighting on the right wing to keep the Prussians away. Even so, by the evening, Wellington's army was wavering and Napoleon called on his last reserve, the famous Imperial Guard, in hope of making the decisive breakthrough.

The French collapse

The Guard had saved the day for Napoleon many times in the past. This time it was stopped in its tracks by the British infantry volleys and turned to run away rather than face the British charge that followed. No one in the French army believed that the Guard could be beaten like that. The shocking, almost unbelievable news of what had happened broke the French will to win. Thousands panicked and fled. The Battle of Waterloo was over.

This time Napoleon was not allowed to make a comeback. He was sent to the lonely island of St. Helena in the South Atlantic, where he died in 1821. He had deliberately kept Europe at war for almost 20 years. He never cared about the human consequences of his actions and was only defeated when his enemies learned to be as brutal as he was. Napoleon had committed the whole of France's resources, both human and economic, to his wars. This would become the pattern for later conflicts.

French cavalry attempts to break into the British infantry squares at the height of the Battle of Waterloo. These unsupported attacks merely wasted Napoleon's cavalry. They were repulsed by the steady fire of the British troops.

THE WAR OF 1812

The United States and Britain were the opposing nations in the War of 1812. Contrary to what the name of the conflict suggests fighting lasted from June 1812 until early 1815. Britain and the United States had various quarrels. Most centered around friction between Britain's continued control of the seas and the United States's hopes to dominate North America. It was President James Madison and a group in the U.S. Congress known as the "War Hawks" who finally used these problems as a reason to declare war.

U.S. regulars take on a force of British infantry and Canadian militia at the Battle of Queenston Heights, on October 13, 1812.

Britain had angered the United States by placing restrictions on U.S. trade as part of its continuing naval war with France during the wars against Napoleon. British warships also regularly drafted sailors from U.S. ships at gunpoint, claiming that the men concerned were British subjects or had deserted from the British navy. Some of them were probably British but several thousand

were U.S. citizens. The right for U.S. vessels to sail the North Atlantic unhindered was therefore the official reason for America's decision to declare war on June 19, 1812.

The War Hawks' real motive, however, was to gain territory for the United States from Canada, which was a British possession. The boundary between the two countries had been in dispute since the end of the American Revolution in 1783. The border was already an area of friction. Britain and Canada had also supported the Shawnee chief Tecumseh in his attacks against U.S. settlers in the Indiana and Ohio areas. The Shawnees had been defeated at the Battle of Tippecanoe in 1811 but Tecumseh would support the British in the coming war.

Failed attacks against Canada

The U.S. leaders began the war with a three-pronged attack on Canada. All three parts of the strategy went wrong. In the west in August 1812 the British and their Native American allies captured Fort Dearborn (the site of present-day Chicago) and Detroit. On the central front, near Lakes Erie and Ontario, a force of over 3,000 U.S. troops suffered about 1,000 dead and taken prisoner in the Battle of Queenston Heights in October; the British lost 14 killed. In the east, near Lake Champlain, U.S. forces pulled back in November without even fighting a battle.

U.S. Secretary of War John Armstrong planned another invasion of Canada in 1813. This was not very successful either. An American force briefly occupied York (now Toronto) early in the year but in the fall an advance toward Montreal finished disastrously. The year ended instead with the British capturing Fort Niagara and burning the town of Buffalo in upstate New York.

There was some better news from the west, however. U.S. troops commanded by General William Henry Harrison recaptured Detroit on September 29, 1813, then routed a British and Native American force at the Battle of the Thames River. Tecumseh was killed.

Harrison's advance was made possible by the U.S. naval victory in the Battle of Lake Erie on September 10. Both sides used the Great Lakes to transport their supplies and men, and each had

U.S. General Andrew Jackson was a supporter of the "War Hawks" who were eager to go to war with the British in 1812. Jackson, later U.S. president, also commanded the U.S. forces at the Battle of New Orleans in January 1815.

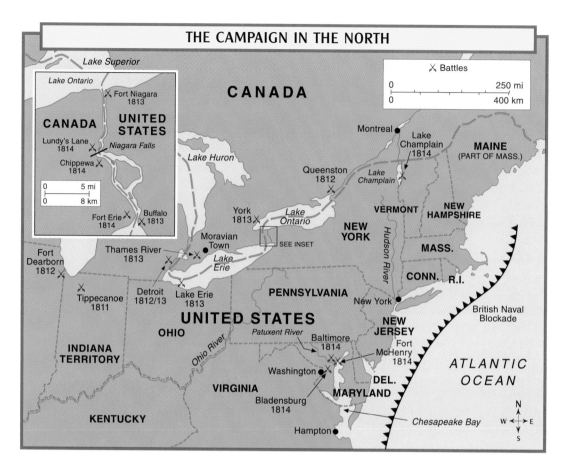

THE CAMPAIGN IN THE NORTH

Much of the War of 1812 was fought along the border between Canada and the United States.

built up squadrons of warships and gunboats. The U.S. commander on Lake Erie was Captain Oliver Hazard Perry. His aggressive leadership won the day. All six British ships surrendered to the nine American vessels. Perry was able to signal to his superiors, "We have met the enemy and they are ours."

Britain strikes back

Despite this defeat the British were able to go on the offensive in 1814. The temporary end of the war against Napoleon in Europe meant that the British were able to ship some of their veteran soldiers across the Atlantic to reinforce their troops in Canada. They began other attacks in the Chesapeake Bay area and later against the important port of New Orleans.

There were two important battles on the Niagara front in July 1814, at Chippewa and Lundy's Lane, and more fighting around Fort Erie in September. Neither side gained a decisive advantage.

THE BATTLE OF LAKE CHAMPLAIN

Control of Lake Champlain was a vital element in the fighting of 1814 because both sides needed to be able to move their supplies and men by boat to avoid the difficult terrain of upstate New York. British forces on land were much stronger but they could not advance unless they also controlled the lake.

The naval forces were almost exactly balanced. Each side had four larger ships and 12 small gunboats, carrying about 100 cannon and 900 men altogether. The U.S. vessels were led by Thomas Macdonough, an experienced officer who knew the lake well. Many of the British crews under George Downie were inexperienced militiamen.

The Americans were at anchor when the British attacked on September 11 and a point-blank two-hour battle followed. The two sides battered each other unmercifully but eventually Macdonough was able to maneuver his own ship to a dominating position. Finally all the ships in the wrecked British squadron surrendered. The U.S. victory saved the country from an invasion potentially far more dangerous than any the British had mounted during the American Revolution.

The British advance along Lake Champlain was more threatening. Over 10,000 British troops planned to advance down the Hudson River. There were less than 5,000 U.S. troops to oppose them. Both sides were supported by a squadron of ships on Lake Champlain, but the Americans were a little stronger. The U.S. victory in the Battle of Lake Champlain on September 11 proved decisive. The British gave up their invasion attempt.

Fort McHenry stands alone

The British had more success in their landings in Chesapeake Bay. Some 5,000 troops went ashore from the Patuxent River on August 19 and then began the 40-mile (64-km) advance to Washington. They won the Battle of Bladensburg on the outskirts of the capital on the 24th, entered the capital, and burned the public buildings in the city before they withdrew a few days later. They attacked Baltimore between September 12 and 14 but the determined American defense forced them to retreat. The

heroic acts of the U.S. garrison of Fort McHenry opposite Baltimore inspired Francis Scott Key to write "The Star-Spangled Banner."

Neither side was now really likely to achieve a decisive victory. The British were disappointed by the failure of their main advance down Lake Champlain. The U.S. economy was suffering and the government was virtually bankrupt. Both sides wanted peace and negotiations began.

The war at sea

The reasons for the U.S.'s economic problems lay in the events of the war at sea. Britain had over 1,000 warships and the U.S. Navy had only 14 at the start of the war. The U.S. Navy did far better than this ratio might suggest because its ships were very well designed for solo raiding operations against British trade. The U.S. ships were also individually more powerful than most of the escort vessels the British used for trade protection.

U.S. ships did capture more than 800 British merchant vessels in the course of the war. There were about 16 minor naval battles, usually with one ship on each side,

U.S. composer Francis Scott Key (top) spots the U.S. flag still flying above Fort McHenry outside Baltimore after a failed bombardment by British warships in September 1814. The scene inspired him to write "The Star-Spangled Banner."

in locations as far apart as the southern Pacific Ocean, the Mediterranean, and the English Channel. U.S. ships won almost all of them. Despite these embarrassments the British maintained a complete blockade of U.S. ports, cutting off all trade. The United States won the individual ship-to-ship naval battles but Britain, with its larger navy, won the war at sea.

Fighting after the war ends

The Treaty of Ghent was agreed upon on December 24, 1814. The news took until early February 1815 to travel to the United States. Neither side really gained or lost by the settlement. It was an apt comment on the war that, because of the time it took for news to travel, the battle for New Orleans on January 8 and several naval engagements were fought after the war was over.

THE BATTLE OF NEW ORLEANS

After the failed attack on Baltimore in September 1814, the British commanders decided to continue their operations with a move against New Orleans. The U.S. government guessed what the British were planning and sent a Tennessee militia general, Andrew Jackson, to take command of the defenses.

The British deployed 7,500 tough veteran soldiers under the experienced General Thomas Pakenham, who began landing at Bayou Bienvenu on December 23. Jackson had only about 5,500 men to defend the town and over 2,000 of them were untrained militiamen.

The British made some halfhearted attempts to get around the American defenses but then Pakenham stupidly decided to make a direct frontal attack. Protected behind earthworks and piles of timber and cotton bales, the defenders shot the British infantry to pieces.

Well over 2,000 British soldiers were killed or wounded; there were about 60 American casualties. Pakenham was one of the British dead.

Although peace terms had already been agreed on before the battle, the news had yet to reach the United States. New Orleans was a particularly pointless battle.

British infantry attempts to cross the ditch in front of the U.S. defenses at the Battle of New Orleans.

U.S. Expansionist Wars

After the end of the American Revolution in 1783 settlers in the United States continued to try to expand their lands inland to the west. During the next century Native American tribes would fight many wars to oppose this expansion but with little lasting success. For the first 50 years most of these wars were fought east of the Mississippi River, in the Ohio area, and in Florida. In the southwest Mexico was the target. At the same time the United States began to project its power across the globe through the U.S. Navy.

U.S cavalrymen charge against their Native American foes during the Battle of the Thames River in 1813. Tecumseh, the leader of the Native Americans, was killed in the fighting.

In 1809 the governor of the Northwest Territory, William Henry Harrison, bought large areas of land in Indiana and Illinois from various groups of Native Americans. Other Native Americans opposed this, saying that the land belonged to Native American people as a whole and that no one had any right to sell it.

The Native Americans against the land sale were led by twin brothers from the Shawnee people, Tecumseh and Tenskwatawa. In 1811 Tenskwatawa fought a battle at Tippecanoe (see page 57) against U.S. troops under Harrison. The battle was indecisive

but Harrison's troops destroyed the main Indian town (Prophetstown) shortly after. Tecumseh joined the British in the War of 1812. Tecumseh had hoped to unite with the Creek people of Georgia and Alabama, who had also supported the British.

Tecumseh, however was killed at the Battle of the Thames (see page 57) on October 5, 1813. The 900 warriors of the main Creek army were almost completely wiped out in the Battle of Horseshoe Bend in what is now eastern Alabama, on March 27, 1814, by 2,000 militiamen under General Andrew Jackson. The Creeks signed a treaty and gave up all their best land.

Wars at home and overseas

Even before the naval successes of the War of 1812 the United States had been sending its military forces to other parts of the world. French interference with U.S. trading ships led to the so-called Quasi War with France between 1798 and 1800. Ships of the new U.S. Navy (established in 1794) fought several successful battles in the Caribbean before the dispute was ended.

The Tripolitan War between 1801 and 1805 was a more serious conflict. For hundreds of years the Barbary States of North Africa—Algiers, Tripoli, Tunis, and Morocco—had been involved

A scene from the Tripolitan War fought between the United States and a number of North African states that openly engaged in piracy in the early 1800s. Here, U.S. naval forces led by Lieutenant Stephen Decatur storm a pirate warship on August 3, 1804.

in piracy. Foreign ships passing their coasts were regularly captured and their crews and passengers enslaved. The U.S. and European nations tried to control this problem by paying local rulers money. In 1801 President Thomas Jefferson decided to send a naval expedition to punish Tripoli.

The U.S. force did not achieve anything until Commodore Edward Preble took command in 1803. Preble hunted many of the pirates down. One of his officers, Stephen Decatur, even raided the harbor of Tripoli to burn a U.S. ship, the *Philadelphia*, that had been captured after it had run aground on a reef a little distance outside the port's harbor. The fighting ended in 1805 and the United States stopped paying tribute to Tripoli. Decatur returned to the region to command U.S. forces in 1815. He forced Algiers to end its attacks on American ships.

Native American wars remained a fact of life at home in the United States. The Seminoles of Florida were the most difficult for the U.S. government to defeat, fighting in 1818, again

THE SEMINOLE WARS

The Seminoles, who mainly lived in Florida, were also victims of U.S. expansionism in the early 19th century. The Seminoles had sided with the British during the War of 1812. They continued to mount raids into Georgia and help escaped slaves after that war ended.

Serious fighting began in 1818 and General Andrew Jackson was put in command of U.S. forces. Even though Florida was part of a Spanish colony, Jackson decided to invade in April 1818. Jackson's men destroyed many of the Seminole villages and he himself led a detachment to capture the Spanish capital at Pensacola on May 24. The United States then made a treaty with Spain to take over Florida and the power of the Seminole people was subdued for some years.

The Second Seminole War broke out in 1835 when the U.S. government tried to resettle the Seminoles in the Indian Territory (now Oklahoma). Led by Osceola, the Seminoles struck back. Colonel Zachary Taylor led the U.S. forces. In 1837 Osceola was captured by the Americans when he was tricked into attending fake peace talks. He died in prison.

Taylor's men also won the important Battle of Lake Okeechobee on Christmas Day 1837 but the Seminoles continued a guerrilla campaign into 1843. Eventually most of the Seminoles were captured and transported to the Indian Territory.

U.S. Marines come under ambush by the Seminoles during the War of 1812. The Seminoles had sided with the British.

between 1835 and 1843, and again between 1856 and 1858. In addition there was the Black Hawk War of 1832. Black Hawk was a leader of the Sauk and Fox people whose lands were in Illinois. Black Hawk was defeated in the Battle of the Bad Axe in August 1832 in what is now eastern Michigan. Under the treaty that ended the war, the survivors were forced to move to Iowa.

Rapid U.S. expansion

Vast areas of what are now the western and southern United States were still European colonies in 1800. The United States bought much of the Mississippi River basin from France in the Louisiana Purchase in 1803—Napoleon was desperate for money to finance his wars against other European countries. The U.S. also acquired Florida and the Pacific Northwest from Spain by the Adams–Onís Treaty in 1819. Mexico declared its independence from Spain in 1821 and retained control of what is now Texas. This would be the next target for U.S. expansion.

Many U.S. citizens had settled in Texas from the 1820s onward. In late June 1835 they began a rebellion against the Mexican government of President Antonio López de Santa Anna. The U.S. citizens wanted to break away from Mexico and intended that Texas should become part of the United States.

Defending the Alamo

The Texans did not have an army but some settlers volunteered to fight for independence, along with a number of men from existing U.S. states. The army, never more than about 1,000 men, also included a number of deserters from the U.S. regular army. However, the Mexican army was far larger than any force the Texans could put into the field. It also had more cavalry and artillery. To the outsider it looked as if the fight for Texan independence was doomed from the start.

Santa Anna attacked the Texan rebels in 1836 but his advance at the head of an army of about 5,000 troops was delayed by the resistance of the small garrison at the Alamo, a deserted mission station at the time a little way outside San Antonio. Although the Alamo's defenders were eventually overwhelmed by sheer numbers, their resolve gave fresh heart to the cause of Texan independence. In the meantime the Texans declared an independent Republic of Texas on March 2.

Independence won at San Jacinto

Sam Houston, a former governor of Tennessee, took command of the main Texas army, which was training volunteers and gathering supplies while the Alamo garrison was fighting to buy time. Houston's 750 men defeated Santa Anna's 1,700 in a surprise attack at San Jacinto, near Galveston Bay, on April 21, 1836.

The Texan forces charged straight at the Mexicans and the one-sided battle lasted just 18 minutes. When the fighting was over, some 800 Mexicans lay dead out of the 1,700 who had fought for Santa Anna. The Texas army, which caught the Mexicans almost completely unprepared for battle, went into action shouting "Remember the Alamo" in memory of the nearly 200 Texans who had been massacred when the mission at San Antonio was captured by the Mexicans.

President Santa Anna himself was captured at San Jacinto and agreed to pull all his forces out of the Texas Republic. Houston became the first president of Texas, which remained independent until 1845 when it became part of the United States.

THE ALAMO

The Alamo was the name of a former Spanish mission in San Antonio, Texas. It was the site of the most famous battle of the Texas War of Independence.

On February 23, 1836, General Santa Anna led an army of 5,000 Mexican troops to attack the Alamo. The buildings were defended by 188 men, including two famous frontiersmen, Davy Crockett and James Bowie. Bowie was originally in command, but when he got sick, William Travis took over.

The Mexicans made numerous frantic attacks and bombarded the Alamo continuously with their artillery. Somehow the defenders held out for 13 days and inflicted around 1,500 casualties on the attackers. Finally the attackers broke through on March 6 and massacred all of the garrison, except for the wife and child of one of them, a slave, and a man who claimed to be Mexican.

Despite this outcome the delay and the casualties imposed on Santa Anna's army helped give the rest of the Texan rebels time to organize their forces and win the decisive battle at San Jacinto.

Mexican troops breaking into the Alamo on March 6 meet fierce Texan resistance.

SOUTH AMERICA'S WARS OF LIBERATION

In 1800 almost all of South America was made up of Spanish and Portuguese colonies. But by the 1820s all these territories had fought for and gained their independence. Argentina was the first, becoming effectively independent from 1810, even if the official declaration of independence did not follow until 1816. Paraguay and Uruguay mounted successful revolts in 1811, though Uruguay was taken over by Brazil from 1816. The longest struggle and fiercest fighting of all also began in 1811, this time in Venezuela.

Simón Bolívar (mounted on the white horse) enters Caracas, the capital of Venezuela, in 1821. Bolívar also freed Colombia, Ecuador, and Peru from Spanish control.

Spanish troops had the upper hand at first in Venezuela. The rebel leader, Simón Bolívar, would not give up. In 1819 he attacked the Spanish around Bogotá. On August 7 Bolívar's men captured most of the Spanish army at the Battle of Boyacá. The Battle of Boyacá made the liberation of northern South America certain, though there was more fighting. One of Bolívar's commanders, Antonio José de Sucre, went on to liberate what is now Ecuador after his victory at the Battle of Pichincha in 1822.

Campaigns for independence

The rebellions in Argentina and Chile had a different hero, José de San Martín. In January 1817 he led his army on an epic march across the Andes Mountains into Chile. He defeated the Spanish at Chacabuco on February 12. A further rebel victory in the Battle of the Maipo in April 1818 forced the Spanish to retreat to Peru.

A maverick British naval officer, Thomas Cochrane, then took command of the small rebel navy. He won command of the sea and in September 1820 carried San Martín's army on a seaborne invasion of Peru. Fighting in Peru swayed back and forth until 1824 but by then San Martín had left the rebel side. He had a meeting with Bolívar at Guayaquil, Equador, in July 1822. No one really knows what happened between the two but San Martín decided to quit and retired to Europe.

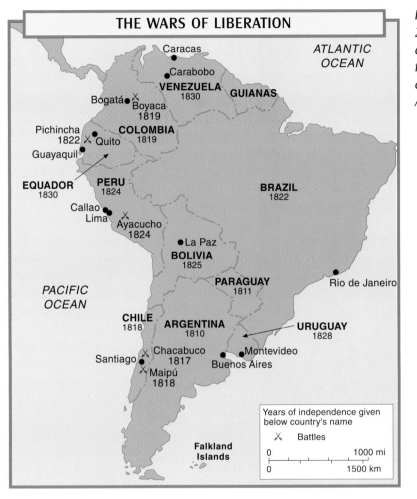

THE WARS OF LIBERATION

Caracas

ATLANTIC OCEAN

Carabobo

VENEZUELA 1830 **GUIANAS**

Bogatá X
Boyaca
1819

Pichincha
1822 X Quito
Guayaquil

COLOMBIA 1819

EQUADOR
1830

PERU
1824

BRAZIL
1822

Callao
Lima X
Ayacucho
1824

● La Paz

BOLIVIA
1825

PARAGUAY
1811

Rio de Janeiro

PACIFIC OCEAN

CHILE
1818 **ARGENTINA**
1810 **URUGUAY**
1828

Santiago X Chacabuco
1817
X Maipú
1818

Montevideo

Buenos Aires

Years of independence given below country's name

X Battles

Falkland Islands

0 ———— 1000 mi
0 ———— 1500 km

In the space of about 20 years the Spanish and Portuguese were forced to give up their colonies in South America.

The Peruvian rebels gained the upper hand in 1824 and Sucre won the decisive victory in the Battle of Ayacucho in Peru in December. His 7,000 men destroyed the 10,000-strong Spanish army. Sixteen Spanish generals and over 2,500 of their men were captured and 1,400 killed. In January 1826, the port of Callao was the last Spanish stronghold in Peru to surrender.

In the meantime Brazil had also defeated its colonial master but with a very different kind of rebellion. Brazil was ruled for Portugal by one of King John VI's sons, Dom Pedro. In 1822 Dom Pedro declared independence from his father and became Emperor Pedro I. Cochrane moved to take command of Pedro's navy and ensured Brazil's independence by his naval victories over Portugal along the Brazilian coast in 1823.

THE U.S.–MEXICAN WAR

Mexico declared war on the United States on April 23, 1846. Fighting began on April 25, when a force of Mexican troops crossed the Rio Grande near its mouth and attacked a U.S. detachment a little way to the north. The U.S. declared war on Mexico on May 13. The causes of the war dated back at least ten years to the Texas declaration of independence in 1836. Mexico never recognized Texan independence. The United States, however, was also intent on grabbing new territory from Mexico.

The idea of allowing Texas to join the United States was also controversial within the United States itself. Slave-owning was legal in Texas and antislavery forces in the United States did not want another slave state to be added to a country that already had several such states. However, President James Polk had won the 1844 election because of his strongly expansionist policies. In 1845 the United States did decide to take over Texas, which U.S. citizens living in Texas also wanted.

A strong line

Mexico had been in a state of upheaval for some years and at the end of 1845 a new Mexican president was ready to take a firm line with the United States. Polk ordered a strong U.S. force to move close to the Texas border with Mexico. This force was attacked near Matamoros on April 25. Some people believe that the U.S. provoked the war; others think that Mexico would have gone to war anyway because of the American takeover of Texas.

U.S regular troops of the type that fought in the war against Mexico. In reality, their clothing would have been torn and dirty on campaign.

Whichever was the case, there was more fighting near the Rio Grande, even before news of the first attack reached Washington. Some 6,000 Mexican troops made these first attacks and they were opposed by 3,500 U.S. troops commanded by General Zachary Taylor. Taylor and his men won two battles in the first days of May at Palo Alto and Resaca de la Palma.

A delayed advance

A long lull followed. On the U.S. side this was because Taylor was busy building up his forces. On the Mexican side a series of rebellions broke out against the government. These ended with the return of the former dictator, General Santa Anna, from exile. The U.S. Navy could have stopped Santa Anna. To be allowed through, he told Polk that he would try to make peace, but this promise was forgotten as soon as he was back in Mexico.

By August 1846 Taylor was ready to advance from his base at Camp Texas (now Brownsville). His target was the town of Monterrey, about 160 miles (256 km) away. Taylor took 6,000 men with him; the Mexican garrison of Monterrey was about 10,000 strong. The American attack began on September 20. There was fierce fighting until the 24th, when Taylor and the opposing Mexican commander, General Pedro de Ampudia, agreed to a truce. The Mexicans surrendered the town, but were allowed to take their weapons and supplies with them when they retreated.

Seaborne invasion

Polk did not approve of the deal that Taylor had made with the Mexicans and ordered him to resume the war. Taylor advanced another 50 miles (80 km) to Saltillo, where he was reinforced by 3,000 troops who had made a difficult 600-mile (960-km) march from San Antonio in Texas.

ZACHARY TAYLOR

Zachary Taylor was one of the leading U.S. commanders in the Mexican War and became the 12th president of the United States in 1849. Before the Mexican War, Taylor had extensive experience of Native American fighting dating back as far as his time as a young soldier in the War of 1812. Later he served in the Black Hawk War of 1832 and in the Second Seminole War during 1837 and 1838.

Taylor was given command of 3,500 U.S. regulars and sent to the Texas border in March 1846. This was a big responsibility because his command was about half of the strength of the entire U.S. Army at that time. Taylor won important early victories and then a major battle at Buena Vista in 1847. This victory made him famous and popular enough to win the 1848 presidential election as the Whig Party candidate.

Taylor died in 1850. One of the nation's greatest problems in his 16 months in office was whether the territories won from Mexico during the war should become free or slave states.

The U.S. leaders now developed a new strategy. They decided that difficult desert terrain would make it impossible for Taylor to advance any farther. Instead the main U.S. attack would be made by sea to the port of Veracruz and from there inland to Mexico City. Taylor's force was cut back to only 5,000 men with the others being sent to join the new expedition.

War in California

Santa Anna thought this gave him the chance to attack and beat Taylor's force before the Veracruz operation began. The result was a Mexican defeat in the Battle of Buena Vista on February 22–23, 1847. This U.S. victory was the last important fighting of the war in northern Mexico.

By the time the U.S.–Mexican War began, many U.S. citizens had already settled in California and in various parts of New Mexico, even though these areas were still Mexican territory. Various small-scale actions during the war were fought in both California and New Mexico.

The settlers in California actually began fighting even before they heard that the United States and Mexico had definitely gone to war. In June 1846 settlers in the Sacramento Valley captured the town of Sonoma and declared a new republic, usually called the Bear Flag Republic after the symbol used on its flag. Captain John C. Frémont happened to be in California with a small U.S. exploring expedition and was named as the republic's president.

In July the settlers discovered that a U.S. Navy force had captured Monterey and claimed California for the United States. A new U.S. Navy commander, Commodore Robert Stockton, then landed more troops at San Diego, Los Angeles, and Santa Barbara in August.

Marching into Mexico and California

In the meantime another U.S. force was on the march through New Mexico. General Stephen Watts Kearny set off along the Santa Fe Trail from Fort Leavenworth, now in Kansas, with about 1,700 Missouri volunteers in June 1846. His orders were to occupy New Mexico and California. Kearny and his small force reached Santa Fe without a fight in August.

Kearny decided to split his force into three groups. One group remained to control New Mexico and fought several skirmishes before gaining the upper hand early in 1847. A second force marched south into Mexico's Chihuahua province. Eventually

THE BATTLE OF BUENA VISTA

In early 1847 the U.S. force's main base in northern Mexico was at the town of Saltillo. General Zachary Taylor's garrison had about 5,000 men. The Mexican commander, General Santa Anna, attacked with about 14,000 troops. Taylor was warned of Santa Anna's advance and decided to defend the hills crossed by a mountain road a few miles to the south.

The two-day battle that followed saw a series of complicated maneuvers and much fierce fighting. First one side seemed to be on top, then the other side gained the upper hand. Several regular army artillery batteries were the backbone of the U.S. defense but a volunteer infantry regiment, the 1st Mississippi Volunteers commanded by Colonel Jefferson Davis, made the vital charge to complete the American victory. The Mexicans retreated with about 1,600 casualties; the U.S. force had about 750 dead, wounded, or missing.

A view of the two-day Battle of Buena Vista showing a charge by U.S. cavalry (left) and artillery firing on the Mexicans (right). Rival infantry also exchange musket fire.

WINFIELD SCOTT

U.S. General Winfield Scott was in charge of the successful advance against the enemy capital, Mexico City, and won several key battles.

General Winfield Scott was the senior general in the U.S. Army at the outbreak of the Mexican War. In November 1846 President Polk sent him to take command of the force heading for Veracruz, which was to undertake the main U.S. offensive of the war against Mexico.

Scott first became famous during the War of 1812 against the British when he was decorated and promoted for his bravery in battle. Like most of the rest of the regular U.S. Army he fought in various Native American wars including those against Black Hawk and the Seminoles. He also wrote a new set of army regulations and was given the nickname "Old Fuss and Feathers" because he thought soldiers' neatness and discipline were so important.

Scott led his small army brilliantly during the capture of Mexico City in 1847 but casualties were very high partly because of the strength of the Mexican forces they faced. After the end of the Mexican War, Scott stood unsuccessfully for the presidency in 1852. He finally retired from the army as its commander-in-chief in 1861, shortly after the outbreak of the Civil War.

they joined up with Taylor's army in northern Mexico after fighting and winning a battle on the way. Kearny himself led the third and smallest group on into California.

When Kearny arrived in California he found that the Mexican population had regained control of much of the state from the U.S. forces. Kearny and his men fought the indecisive Battle of San Pascual near San Diego on December 6, and then joined up with the U.S. Navy forces under Stockton to win the decisive Battle of San Gabriel on January 9, 1847. This clear-cut U.S. victory ended the fighting in California.

By then the main U.S. offensive was ready to start. General Winfield Scott established a forward base at Tampico on the Mexican coast in February 1847, before moving farther south to begin landings near Veracruz on March 9. He quickly surrounded the town. It surrendered on March 27, following a five-day naval and land bombardment.

On to Mexico City

Scott then led his 10,000 troops inland. General Santa Anna stood ready to block their advance with some 12,000 Mexican troops at Cerro Gordo, 50 miles (80 km) from the coast. Some of Scott's officers managed to scout a little-known mountain road and so he was able to surround part of the Mexican force. The Battle of Cerro Gordo was fought on April 18. Mexican casualties were over 4,000 men while the U.S. force lost about 400.

By mid-May Scott's advance had pushed on to Puebla, about 80 miles (128 km) from Mexico City, but could go no farther. Many of his men had fallen sick and he had to allow others to go

U.S. General Winfield Scott (left) oversees the bombardment of the Mexican port of Veracruz in March 1847. After five days under fire, the Mexican garrison surrendered.

U.S troops fire on the Mexican front line at the height of the Battle of Molino del Rey, September 8, 1847. After heavy fighting for a foundry and an old fort (center right), the Mexicans fled.

home because their time in the army had expired. By August Scott still had over 3,000 sick, but reinforcements had brought his effective force up to about 11,000. Scott decided to leave the sick in Puebla, with a small garrison to protect them, while he led the main army on toward the Mexican capital.

Mexico surrenders

Santa Anna had about 30,000 troops left under his command but did not resist Scott's advance strongly until it reached Contreras, about 10 miles (16 km) south of the capital city, on August 19. There was more fighting there and at Churubusco nearby the next day. U.S. losses were very heavy at over 1,000 killed and wounded but the Mexican casualties were far worse—4,500 killed and wounded and over 2,500 prisoners. Many Mexican troops also deserted.

Scott agreed to stop fighting for almost two weeks after this battle to try to negotiate a peace deal. When negotiations failed, he attacked again. There were two further battles, at Molino del Rey on September 8 and at Chapultepec on September 13. Both were U.S. victories. Mexico City fell on the 14th.

The war was effectively over with the capture of Mexico City, though it took until well into 1848 for the Treaty of Guadalupe Hidalgo to be agreed to by both governments. Mexico recognized the Rio Grande as the southern boundary of Texas and gave up the whole of California and New Mexico (including the modern states of Nevada, Utah, Arizona, and parts of Colorado and Wyoming) to the United States.

The U.S. war against Mexico was waged over a large portion of southwestern North America but the key campaign was that led by Winfield Scott from Veracruz to Mexico City.

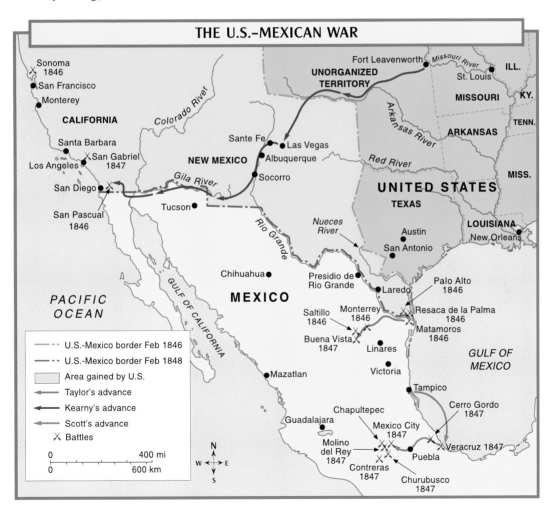

THE U.S.–MEXICAN WAR

GLOSSARY

broadside A naval term describing the simultaneous firing of all the cannon on one side of a warship. Cannon were arranged on decks, one above the other. The greater the number of decks, the larger the ship and heavier its broadside.

conscription The process by which citizens of a country are legally required to serve in its armed forces. Countries can have conscription in both peacetime and in war.

corps A large force of soldiers of between 20,000 and 30,000 men. Corps could consist of just cavalry or infantry, but they more usually contained both cavalry and infantry, as well as artillery. A corps was large enough and had the range of troops and weapons to fight a full-scale battle alone if needed. Two or more corps would combine to build an army.

division The basic building block of a corps, a division consisted of two or three brigades of soldiers of the same type. A brigade contained three to five regiments each of approximately 1,000 men, giving a division a strength of approximately 10,000 soldiers.

light infantry Soldiers who did not usually fight in close-packed lines or columns. They fought from behind cover or widely spaced, and were trained to show personal initiative rather than blindly follow orders. Most were above-average shots.

square A defensive formation adopted by foot soldiers when threatened by cavalry. The soldiers fixed bayonets, faced outward, and fired at the cavalrymen as they charged. Cavalry charges were rarely able to break into a square. Squares were, however, very slow moving and especially vulnerable to artillery fire because they made a large, usually stationary target.

volunteer An individual who becomes a soldier of his own free will. People volunteer to fight for many reasons, such as patriotism, the pursuit of glory, or even the food, money, and shelter offered by an army.

BIBLIOGRAPHY

Note: An asterisk (*) denotes a Young Adult title.

*Bovert, Howard E., et al. *Book of the American Revolution*. Little, Brown, 1994

*Davis, Burke. *Black Heroes of the American Revolution*. Harcourt Brace, 1992

Dupuy, R. Ernest and Dupuy, Trevor. *The Collins Encyclopedia of Military History*. HarperCollins, 1993

Dupuy, R.E., Johnson, Curt, and Bongard, David L. *The Harper Encyclopedia of Military Biography*. HarperCollins, 1995

*Fleming, Thomas. *Liberty!: The American Revolution*. Viking, 1997

*Lind, Michael. *The Alamo: An Epic*. Houghton, 1997

*Mills, Bronwhy. *The Mexican War*, "America at War" series. Facts on File, 1992

Muir, Rory. *Tactics and the Experience of Battle in the Age of Napoleon*. Yale University, 1998.

*Rosenburg, John. *First in War: George Washington in the American Revolution*. Milbrook Press, 1998

*Sugden, John. *Tecumseh: A Life*. Macrae Books, 1998

White, Colin. *The Nelson Companion*. Annapolis Naval Institute, 1997.

*Zeinert, Karen. *Those Remarkable Women of the American Revolution*. Millbrook Press, 1996

INDEX

ACKNOWLEDGMENTS

Cover (main picture) Collection of the Monmouth Court Historical Association (Gift of the Descendants of David Leavitt, 1937), (inset) Peter Newark's Military Pictures; page 1 AKG Photo, London; page 5 Peter Newark's American Pictures; page 8 Peter Newark's Military Pictures; page 9 Robert Hunt Library; page 11 Peter Newark's American Pictures; page 12 Peter Newark's Military Pictures page 13 Peter Newark's Historical Pictures; page 15 Robert Hunt Library; page 16 Robert Hunt Library; page 18 AKG Photo, London; page 21 Peter Newark's Military Pictures; page 22 Peter Newark's Military Pictures; page 24 Peter Newark's Military Pictures; page 25 AKG Photo, London; page 26 AKG Photo, London; page 27 AKG Photo, London; page 30 Peter Newark's Military Pictures; page 31 AKG Photo, London; page 32 AKG Photo, London; page 34 Peter Newark's Historical Pictures; page 36 Peter Newark's Military Pictures; page 37 AKG Photo, London; page 38 Peter Newark's Military Pictures; page 41 Peter Newark's Military Pictures; page 42 Peter Newark's Military Pictures; page 45 AKG Photo, London; page 47 Peter Newark's Military Pictures; page 48 AKG Photo, London; page 51 Peter Newark's Military Pictures; page 52 Peter Newark's Military Pictures; page 55 AKG Photo, London; page 56 Peter Newark's Military Pictures; page 57 Peter Newark's American Pictures; page 60 Peter Newark's American Pictures; page 61 Peter Newark's Military Pictures; page 62 Peter Newark's American Pictures; page 63 Peter Newark's American Pictures; page 65 Peter Newark's Military Pictures; page 67 Peter Newark's Military Pictures; page 68 AKG Photo, London; page 70 Peter Newark's Military Pictures; page 73 Peter Newark's Military Pictures; page 74 Peter Newark's American Pictures; page 75 AKG Photo, London; page 76 Peter Newark's Military Pictures.